The Essential Guide to
Kinship
Care

Trauma-Informed, Practical Help for You and Your Family

Sarah Naish and Enza Smith

Jessica Kingsley Publishers
London and Philadelphia

First published in Great Britain in 2025 by Jessica Kingsley Publishers
An imprint of John Murray Press

2

A CIP catalogue record for this title is available from
the British Library and the Library of Congress

ISBN 978 1 80501 281 8
eISBN 978 1 80501 282 5

Printed and bound in Great Britain by Clays Ltd, Elcograf S.p.A.

Jessica Kingsley Publishers' policy is to use papers that are natural,
renewable and recyclable products and made from wood grown in
sustainable forests. The logging and manufacturing processes are expected
to conform to the environmental regulations of the country of origin.

Jessica Kingsley Publishers
Carmelite House
50 Victoria Embankment
London EC4Y 0DZ

www.jkp.com

John Murray Press
Part of Hodder & Stoughton Ltd
An Hachette Company

The authorised representative in the EEA is Hachette Ireland,
8 Castlecourt Centre, Dublin 15, D15 XTP3, Ireland (email: info@hbgi.ie)

The Essential Guide to
Kinship Care

from the author

The A–Z of Therapeutic Parenting
Strategies and Solutions
Sarah Naish
ISBN 978 1 78592 376 0
eISBN 978 1 78450 732 9
Audiobook ISBN 978 1 52937 496 4

The A–Z of Survival Strategies
for Therapeutic Parents
From Chaos to Cake
Sarah Naish
Illustrated by Kath Grimshaw
ISBN 978 1 83997 172 3
eISBN 978 1 83997 173 0
Audiobook ISBN 978 1 39980 419 6

Contents

Introduction

Welcome to a small dose of clarity! So necessary in the shifting sands of kinship care, kinship fostering and special guardianship.

We know that life can be very confusing, and questions are perhaps coming at you from all angles. Or maybe there is the distinct sound of tumbleweed where vital information *should* be! To make things more difficult, your experience will vary depending on:

- where you live
- the child's individual circumstances
- your relationship with the birth parents
- your relationship to the child
- your own personal circumstances.

Why We Wrote This Book

Through our work, we have often found that kinship carers have been left in the dark and confused by all the different options that might be open to them. It seems to us that this sector is less well supported than adopters and foster parents, and there was a definite book-shaped space needing to be filled with all the concise and essential information that you require.

Perhaps you are a grandparent, aunt, uncle or other related person, who has suddenly found themselves in a situation where you have been asked to care for a child you know, or perhaps you don't know them but are related to – a 'connected child'. This can throw your life, and everything in it, up in the air.

Or maybe you are a foster carer or family friend who knows the child well, and you have been asked to become a special guardian.

Increasingly, foster carers are also choosing to become kinship carers and take out a Special Guardianship Order (SGO) for a child they have known for some time. Often, they feel unsupported once the order has been granted.

We understand that trying to make sense of a rapidly changing situation can be overwhelming. You need a concise guide to help you navigate it all.

This book breaks down each challenge you may face into easy-to-understand sections, giving you the tools to help you make informed decisions. Please believe us when we say you are not alone. An estimated 200,000 children live with kinship carers across the UK.

How to Use This Book

We know you don't have a lot of time, so we've made this book easy for you to dip in and out of. Some of the sections won't apply to you yet, or perhaps they never will. You don't have to read this book in order; you can skip through and pick out the bits that you need.

At the beginning of some sections, we identify whether it is Sarah Naish or Enza Smith writing. This relates to the sharing of personal experiences.

You will find that we often provide links for helpful organizations and also ways in which you can make contact with others in a similar situation.

As well as practical advice around legal orders and assessment, we also deal with the emotional side, the isolation of kinship care and how looking after a child who may have suffered trauma is different from looking after a securely attached child.

You might find that some of the book is relevant now and then some sections will be relevant later on. Either way, we hope this will become your go-to easy-access comforting friend.

About the Authors

Sarah Naish is an adopter of five children and is a former social worker. She has direct experience of changes within her own family which led to a kinship care arrangement taking place. Through her work at the Centre of Excellence in Child Trauma, Sarah has been very involved in supporting kinship carers and other therapeutic parents such as adopters and foster parents. Her main task in this book has been to provide information about managing the many changes, especially relating to changing relationships, therapeutic parenting and caring for a child who has experienced trauma.

Enza Smith MBE has dedicated 25 years of her life to being a kinship carer. She has extensive experience of being a special guardian as well as experience of a Child Arrangement Order and the care system. In 2011, she founded Kinship Carers UK, a grassroots charity that provides vital support to kinship carers regardless of their legal orders. Enza's relentless work has helped countless carers, and through her work, she has realized the necessity of providing vital information to assist them in navigating the complexities of kinship care. Her goal within this book is to use her extensive knowledge to empower both new and existing kinship carers by providing valuable information for a better future.

What Is Kinship Care?

Sadly, it's relatively common for children to find themselves in situations where they cannot live with their birth parents, for various reasons. Thankfully, relatives and friends step in to provide kinship care. These relatives include grandparents, siblings, aunts and uncles, other extended family members and close family friends. These compassionate carers are called family and friend carers, and they make a massive difference in the lives of the children they care for.

You may well be a new kinship carer, or perhaps you have been asked to consider the possibility of becoming one. Maybe you know the child well, and have been looking after them for some time as a foster carer.

When you consider taking on a child under kinship care arrangements, there are a few options, even though this might not be made clear to you at the time. We will explain each route and outline the pros and cons we have experienced. We hope this will take some of the pressure off and help clarify the pathway you may want to take. It's crucial you look at what route is best for you, your family and the child moving into your home, as once you have made your decision, it can be challenging to change the legal order.

The main types of kinship care are:

- private arrangements, sometimes called private fostering
- relative or connected fostering
- Child Arrangement Order (CAO)
- Special Guardianship Order (SGO).

We go into a lot more detail about these different types of kinship care later on. Whichever path you take, it is essential that you understand your options and how things may change in the future. The different sections in this book will help you with that, particularly in Chapter 1, so let's start there!

Initial Impact

Overview

You might just have been told that someone needs you to care for a child. Maybe you know the child, perhaps you are their grandparent. Or maybe the child is connected to someone in your family, but you hardly know them.

You may have a lot of conflicting feelings. Maybe you are relieved that the child is with you, or perhaps you feel resentment at the interference of others. It might all be rather overwhelming.

Whatever the situation, when kinship care (sometimes called family and friends care, or connected care) is sought, it can often come out of the blue. Suddenly there are a whole load of things you need to think about. New routines, equipment, people you don't know and meetings to go to, which might seem never ending or very complicated.

Chapter 1 of this book is designed to help you to navigate some of those immediate hurdles you face. Later on, we will look at issues as they develop, but right now you will need to think about what to do first. Here we will guide you through those challenges.

1A: What Just Happened?

[See also Chapter 3: A Different Child?]

There are many reasons why your connected child might have suddenly come to live with you. It's possible that they are not yet living with you, but you've had a phone call from Social Services or another professional who has spoken to you about a potential need for this to happen.

The event may have come completely out of the blue and be a real shock, or alternatively it might be a situation you've been aware of for some time and have had concerns about. Maybe you've even shared those concerns with others.

Some of the main reasons that children need to move out of their birth parents' homes either temporarily or long term are as follows:

- Bereavement
- Issues with drugs or alcohol
- Child abuse
- Abandonment
- Relationship breakdown
- Mental health problems.

This list is not exhaustive but does highlight most of the areas where kinship carers suddenly find themselves looking after a child.

Abuse is further categorized into four different areas:

- Physical abuse
- Emotional abuse
- Sexual abuse
- Neglect.

Any form of abuse will have caused trauma to the child and this trauma will manifest itself through behaviours and psychological issues. We explain this in Chapter 3 in more detail.

Here are the experiences of two kinship carers:

GRANDMOTHER

Although I had been worried about my daughter's parenting, I never thought it would result in my grandchildren coming to live with me. I suspected that she had mental health problems as she often seemed depressed. I tried to support her the best I could. One day, I had a call at 3am from the police to ask if I could have my grandchildren. Of course, I said yes! I was very worried about my daughter, who had been sectioned and taken to hospital. I was really shocked and upset. Luckily, I had quite a lot of equipment because the children stayed with me a fair bit. The children were very upset and we didn't know what was going on. They both regressed. There didn't seem to be anybody who could help me but there were suddenly lots of jobs I needed to do! I felt as if I was being pulled in lots of different directions all at once.

MATERNAL AUNT

When my sister got pregnant I said how worried I was that she would not be able to look after my nephew because she takes drugs. Social Services listened to me and took us seriously. Once my nephew was born he came to live with us almost straight away. Although we had half expected it, there had been so much uncertainty that in the end we were quite unprepared. I still found myself rushing out and getting equipment because I hadn't had a new baby in the house for several years. The first couple of months were really difficult as nobody seemed to know what was going to happen. Nobody told me about the ways that drugs affect babies while they're in the womb. I had to find that out for myself.

1B: Who Is in Charge?

[See also 2C: What Are My Rights?]

When a child comes to live with you, it can be really confusing working out what you are allowed to do and what you are not. A lot of the answers lie in who holds 'parental responsibility'.

Parental responsibility (PR) is a term that means parents have legal rights and duties relating to a child's upbringing, such as caring for them appropriately, providing medical treatment, deciding where they go to school, choosing a religion and registering or changing their name. Only the courts can remove parental responsibility for adoption or under exceptional circumstances.

Child Arrangement Order

As a kinship carer with a CAO, you are on an equal footing with the child's parents regarding PR. This can be incredibly helpful if you have a good relationship with them. With mutual understanding, you don't need their permission to handle primary care requirements such as school activities, haircuts, dental appointments and GP appointments. However, you should still keep the parents informed about significant health decisions.

Connected foster care

As a kinship connected foster carer, it's important to know that you don't have PR. The local authority has overriding PR, while the child's parents still retain theirs and must be consulted. However, as a carer, you can still parent the child as if they were your own, which includes taking them to medical appointments, enrolling them in clubs and going on holidays together.

Special Guardianship Order

Special Guardianship Orders allow for more decision-making

power without needing parental agreement, and allow the final say in most decisions about the child's upbringing, for example where the child lives or goes to school. There are exceptions, however, such as changing the child's surname, putting the child up for adoption, taking the child abroad for more than three months, and the child having surgery for reasons other than improving health.

Most of us like to keep photographic and video memories of fun times spent with our kinship children, and there is no rule against this unless the child disagrees. Generally, no clear guidelines exist when posting pictures or videos of your kinship children on social media, except for having the child's permission. Talking to the parents to agree on some guidelines is a good idea. If everyone can't agree to these guidelines, you can ask the other to take down any pictures or videos of the child on social media. Local authorities have guidelines in place concerning showing photos or videos of looked-after children on social media platforms, and these rules must be agreed on by everyone involved. There are also privacy laws that may help; for more information, please visit www.kinshipcarersuk.com/faqs.

1C: I Need Stuff!

[See also Chapter 9: It's Not About the Money, but...]

We understand that having a child come to live with you, whether it's planned or an emergency, can be financially challenging. When a child is placed in your care to protect them from harm or significant need, it is important to know you can ask for help to ensure that all their needs are met. The local authority can help meet the needs of your connected child. You may need to buy essential items immediately, such as a cot, nappies, baby milk, food, pushchair, car seat, school uniform, bed, bedding, toiletries, clothing, food, and specialist or safety equipment. Transport can also be supported, for example, for taking the child to school or various appointments or meetings. A kinship carer said:

> We got a call to go and pick up my partner's grandson from the hospital there and then without any warning. We hadn't met him or even knew he existed! The nurse and social worker refused to let him go with Mum as she had hurt him. We didn't hesitate, and he left with a mucky vest, a nappy and a hospital blanket. We drove home with him on my knee, seatbelt around us. He was too exhausted to know what was happening, and we were too scared of repercussions to ask for anything. The social worker knew we had nothing for him at home as I'd never had children. On the way home, we stopped at our local supermarket and bought stuff to get us through the night.

We recommend requesting a written agreement from the social worker that outlines the reimbursement for necessary items to help the child settle in. The agreement should include important details such as the date, time, name of the child/ren and the social worker's name. It's also essential for the social worker to confirm that the local authority will reimburse you for emergency items needed for the child. Don't forget to ask for a list of approved emergency items and the maximum amount authorized by the local authority. Remember to keep all receipts for the items you purchase for the child. We hope this information helps you feel confident and supported as you care for your kinship child.

1D: Essential Things First

[See also 1E: Who Is Everyone?, 2B: What Documents Should I Have?, 8A: Responsibilities and Expectations]

Starting or going through a kinship journey can be overwhelming for anyone, with a lot of information to absorb and questions like who said what, when. It can be challenging to keep track. This is what kinship carers have said:

> During my assessment, I asked about becoming a kinship foster carer for my grandson. The social worker who was assessing me told me that 'this was not a feasible option and my only option was an SGO'. After a few months, I found out that I could have applied to be a foster carer. Had I put my request in writing, it would have been taken into consideration. I spoke to the kinship manager and was told that 'the assessing social worker would not have made such a statement and that I may have misunderstood'. In hindsight, it would have been helpful to document my request in writing, then perhaps my grandson would have had the support he needed and I would have had the money to give him what he deserves.

One helpful tip is maintaining a detailed diary, with space to jot down professional details, names, numbers, dates and times of meetings or phone conversations. It is also recommended to communicate through text messages or emails and not rely too much on phone calls to avoid missing or misinterpreting essential information; sometimes, if the conversation is not recorded, it is hard to prove it was said. If you have a diary, you can also share this information with your social worker to confirm it is correct. Some carers find it helpful to have separate email addresses so emails are easier to find and keep track of.

When my niece Jessica came to live with us at eight months old, she was underweight, still just drinking milk, not knowing how to play and not even sitting up! My sister hadn't even been bothered to fill in her red book. And because of the pandemic, she hadn't even seen a health visitor since leaving the hospital. I registered her with my GP and made appointments with the health visitor. I have even booked Jessie into our nursery and local primary school to make sure she doesn't miss out. I want to give her an excellent start to life, but for now, we are going to the mum and toddler group and getting to know each other.

It is also helpful to have a record of key people who may be involved in your kinship journey; for example:

- your social worker and the child's social worker – contact details, including out-of-hours numbers in case of emergencies
- nursery or school details – address, key workers or assigned teacher names, emails, contact numbers
- GP and health professionals' contact and address details, including school nurse, paediatric doctors, dentist, opticians.

Your little one may not have seen any of the above professionals, so it will be up to you to find the services and book them.

1E: Who Is Everyone?

[See also 8D: Meetings]

At some point during your kinship journey, you will meet and work alongside most of these people. However, for special guardians most of this will not apply.

The people	The roles
Assessing social worker	To complete the viability and full assessment report.
Child and adolescent mental health services (CAMHS)	A team of professionals who support the mental health of children and young adults through multidisciplinary services. They offer a wide range of services such as assessment, treatment and support for both individuals and families.
Supervising social worker	To assist the foster carer in their task of providing care to a child in care.
Children's advocate	To speak on behalf of children who are in the care system. An independent advocate, they will speak to the child and share the child's voice in meetings on their behalf and explain processes and procedures.
Children's social worker (CSW)	To support the children and work with you to make sure their needs are met.
Court Guardian CAFCASS (Children and Family Court Advisory and Support Service)	Appointed by the court to give an independent view of what has happened and what should happen in the child's life.
Emergency Duty Team (EDT)	To operate a call service (open at night and at weekends) and offer support and advice.
Family Drugs and Alcohol Court (FDAC)	To work with court proceedings where birth parents are involved with drugs and alcohol.
Family Group Conference (FGC)	A confidential family meeting to discuss plans for a child. It is independently chaired, and you may bring a friend/advocate. Attendance is not enforceable.
Fostering panel agency decision maker (ADM)	To read your kinship assessment, interview you and your partner and decide about your role as a foster carer.

cont.

The people	The roles
Health visitor (HV)	To work with families with a child aged 0 to five to identify health needs and improve the health and well-being of the child.
Independent reviewing officer (IRO)	To oversee meetings with you and other professionals and ensure that the local authority is compliant by monitoring the child plan.
Looked-after child (LAC)	A child who has been in the care of their local authority for more than 24 hours is known as a looked-after child.
LAC review/meeting	A statutory meeting where carers, key people and professionals meet to plan and discuss the child's progress and make plans. The child/young person can attend.
LAC nurse	To make sure the health needs of looked-after children are met and take part in LAC reviews and professional meetings.
McKenzie Friend	To assist you in court if you do not have a solicitor to provide support and assistance. They do not have to be legally qualified and can either be a friend or a family member. Some charities and support organizations provide McKenzie Friends for free – check at your local family court if a McKenzie Friend can ask permission from the court; they may have to complete a form before they are allowed to enter.
Personal Education Plan (PEP) meetings	Meetings held termly for the child to focus on the child's education and any experiences in the child's life that can impact it. They are attended by the designated teacher (DT), social worker, kinship carer and child, if they wish.
School nurse	To ensure that children receive health assessments and to offer support on various topics, including smoking cessation, healthy eating and weight, relationships, safe sex, and drug and alcohol awareness.

Virtual school head (VSH)	To improve educational outcomes by working with schools, children, carers and professionals to ensure that the educational needs of looked-after and previously looked-after children are met. This could mean funding directed to the child, extracurricular needs or help in class.

1F: Court Glossary and Who You May See in Court

[See also 2D: What Happens at Court, 11C: Legal Challenges]

Glossary of terms

Adjournment	Sometimes, a judge may recommend delaying a hearing, which involves taking a break and continuing the court session at a later time. This is usually suggested if the judge believes it could assist all parties in reaching an agreement or if more time is needed to collect additional evidence or complete the necessary paperwork.
Dispute Resolution Appointment (DRA)	Follows the preparation of expert reports if this is considered likely to be helpful in the child's interests.
Fact-finding hearing	A legal process in which allegations are investigated by presenting evidence and cross-examining parties. The judge makes a decision based on the evidence presented.
Family Drug and Alcohol Court (FDAC)	Works with parents with alcohol and substance misuse issues. The programme encourages collaboration between parents and professionals. The FDAC team provides a recommendation to the court regarding the parent's ability to care for their child, or seeks to remove the child to the care of family and friends, if appropriate.

cont.

First Hearing and Dispute Resolution Appointment (FHDRA)	Used to identify what issues are in dispute between the parties and what steps need to be taken before a final decision, such as getting CAFCASS involved to make a report.
Final hearing	Where the judge orders the legal order and completes the arrangements for the child.
Interim Care Order (ICO)	An order made before a final order, which temporarily puts a child under the local authority's care or supervision. It may be that the child stays with the family or is placed in foster care. Initially, the order lasts eight weeks and can be renewed for 28 days. The local authority acquires parental responsibility for the child.
Litigant in person	Someone who represents themselves and does not have legal representation in the Family Court.
Public Law Outline (PLO)	Sets out the local authority's duties when considering taking a case to court to ask for a care order. If a local authority asks you to a PLO meeting, you will be advised to have legal representation at the meeting and you may try to put in place agreements to avoid court proceedings.
Private law	Court proceedings between parents or extended family members, not involving a local authority and where care proceedings are not being considered.
Public law	Court proceedings where the local authority, via Social Services, makes applications to the court to obtain legal powers to intervene in families.
Supervision order	Gives a local authority legal powers to monitor a child's progress and needs while the child lives at home or elsewhere. Help and support can be given to the family/carers.

Who you may see in court

Advocate	Someone who speaks for you, for example a solicitor.
Applicant	The person making an application, either an individual such as a parent or grandparent, or a public body, such as a local authority.
Barrister/counsel	A lawyer who usually specializes in courtroom representation.
Children and Family Court Advisory and Support Service (CAFCAS)	This body looks after the interests of children when they become involved in family court proceedings.
Court usher	Responsible for ensuring that your hearing goes smoothly. Be sure you inform the usher if you represent yourself or bring a McKenzie Friend into the hearing.
Family Court Judge	Sit in the Family Court and the Family Division of the High Court. They deal with the most complex cases relating to children and families.
Guardian	An individual qualified and experienced in social work and in working with children, appointed by courts to represent the rights and interests of children. They will have their own solicitor/barrister to represent them in any court proceedings.
Magistrate	Also known as Justices of the Peace (JPs), these are volunteers from the local community who are not usually legally qualified but receive ongoing training and have the support of a legal advisor in court.
McKenzie Friend	Having a solicitor by your side is always helpful, but not everyone can afford one. Representing yourself in court may be the only option. It can be challenging, but having a kind, supportive person in court with you can make the process more manageable.

1G: What About the Children?

[See also 4B: What Is Therapeutic (Trauma-Informed) Parenting?]

Whatever has happened, your connected child (or children) is going to have some immediate needs, and it's going to be you who has to meet those needs.

First of all, we want to make sure we establish CPR:

- Consistency
- Predictability
- Reliability.

All children need to have a routine so that they are able to predict the future. Where children have experienced sudden moves or disruption in their lives, the need for that routine is even more important. Perhaps the child has been living in a situation where there was no routine and things changed at a moment's notice? Maybe the parent was unreliable, for whatever reason, and the child now needs to learn that they can rely on you.

It's essential that you say what you mean and mean what you say. The child needs to know that they can count on you.

Sometimes it can be tempting to overshare. Be very careful about what you say in the child's earshot. They will already be worrying about what's happening. The main thing we want to communicate is that whatever has happened, it is not the child's fault. They will be feeling as if it is, and we need to relieve them of that worry.

We also want to make sure that we are able to be as honest as we can be with children. Where the child has been rescued from a very abusive situation, they already *know* the truth anyway. They know what has happened to them. Don't be tempted to collude with the abuser, whoever they may be. Someone's got to be in the child's corner and have the child's perspective. This can be very difficult to manage where there has been an allegation and you are not sure what to think about that allegation.

As long as you are able to establish a strong routine and remain consistent for the child, this will alleviate a lot of their anxiety. Be very clear about what is happening and share information that you can, but don't over promise. For example, if you are hoping the child can visit a parent, don't mention this until you are certain. 'Possibly' or 'maybe' should leave your vocabulary for now.

It's possible that you have not previously known this child. In this case, it is essential that you have information about the child and their birth parents. You need to know the circumstances in which they have come into your care in order to make proper plans. We explain this in more detail in 1B: Who Is In Charge and 1C: I Need Stuff!.

1H: Seeing Birth Parents: Initial Considerations

[See also 1B: Who Is in Charge?, Chapter 5: Family Tensions, Visits and Family Time [Contact]]

It's likely that from the very early days there will be an expectation that your connected child continues to see their birth parents. Social Services usually refer to family visits as 'contact'. It is also referred to as 'contact' in court proceedings. You may want to think about the terminology you use, especially around the child. After all, it is not a common phrase to 'have contact with Mum'!

Later on, in Chapter 5, we look at family visit times in much more detail. Here we are just talking about the early days and what to think about when the supporting professionals around you are trying to arrange for this to happen.

The difficulties might be that your whole routine has now

changed and suddenly you're having to think about finding family centres or perhaps having the birth parents visit you at home when normally that wasn't the case. Sometimes it can feel as if you're under a lot of pressure to accept arrangements which feel uncomfortable or unworkable. It's important to try to be objective about what is feasible and what is in the best interests of the child.

It's not unusual for Social Services to ask kinship carers to supervise the contact, especially where you have a good relationship with the birth parents. Bear in mind that this relationship is likely to come under immense strain over the next few days or weeks, and the situation can change rapidly.

Sometimes, where there are high levels of concerns for the child's safety, or Social Services wish to monitor whether or not the parents are under the influence of drugs or alcohol, they will arrange for the visit to be professionally supervised. It is not unusual for an assistant social worker or support worker to be the person supervising. Sometimes, the supervisor is collecting evidence for court or other reports.

It's a really good idea to ensure that all arrangements are made in writing. Avoid making informal arrangements directly with the birth parents, unless you have been told this is okay. Even then, make sure you have a written record. Things can unravel very fast!

Also start to notice and record any changes in the child's behaviour. We explain what to look out for in 5F: Supporting the Child Around Visits (Contact) With Birth Parents.

There is usually tension around family visits, and the birth parents may not agree with the level which has been set. You may also disagree and feel it is too much or too little. It's important to be really clear about the impact on your own life and how much you can fit in. By the time you have got the child ready, travelled to the venue, waited for the visit to end and travelled back, it can take three to four hours out of your day.

Sometimes arrangements are made through mutual consent,

and sometimes Social Services or the courts will be very prescriptive about arrangements. A lot depends on the child's legal status (i.e. if they are looked after).

1I: Where Can I Go for Help?

[See also 2G: What Support Can I Get?]

Many of us have not experienced kinship care until we get the letter, the call or the knock on the door. It's hard to predict what kind of support we might need in the future. We rely on our past experiences of parenting, and trust that will be enough, as how different can it be? Then, the honeymoon period is over, and the difficulties our kinship children have experienced come flooding out as they begin to trust that they are safe. We start to learn about our kinship children's trauma as they open up to us and feel more secure.

We understand that the path ahead may be challenging, but we want you to know that you are not alone. You can go to your local authority kinship team and ask for an assessment of need. A social worker may investigate and signpost or support you with services such as the Adoption and Special Guardianship Support Fund. However, there are organizations which we recommend, such as Kinship Carers UK and the National Association of Therapeutic Parents (NATP) (part of the Centre of Excellence in Child Trauma).

NATP: A not-for-profit organization which nationally supports anyone who is caring for neurodiverse children and children who have experienced trauma. They run 'Listening Circles' for kinship carers and have a wealth of resources. www.naotp.com.

Kinship Carers UK: A wonderful independent charity run by professional kinship carers for kinship carers. They offer advice from experienced and professional carers who have walked in your shoes, support groups both morning and evening, face-to-face and virtual, and a Kinship Community Café, interviews with professionals working in or with kinship families you may not otherwise know or be in touch with. There are also volunteering opportunities for kinship carers. Tel: 07714 531 802. www.kinshipcarersuk.com.

Other organizations offering advice and support

Adfam: A national charity tackling the adverse effects of drugs and alcohol on family members, offering family support and resources. www.adfam.org.uk.

Buttle UK: Offers grants for children and families in financial hardship. www.buttleuk.org.

CoramBAAF: Offers free children's legal advice and advocacy services. www.corambaaf.org.uk.

Family Rights Group: A well-established charity that advises kinship carers about their rights and options. Free advice line: 0808 801 0366. www.frg.org.uk.

Grandparents Plus (known as Kinship): A government-supported organization that offers services to kinship carers. www.kinship.org.uk.

Kinship Care Northern Ireland: Supporting local kinship carers, offering support and various services to kinship families. www.kinshipcareni.com.

Kinship Care Advice Service for Scotland: Offers free advice, support and services for kinship carers. Helpline: 0808 800 0006. www.kinship.scot.

The Fostering Network: Offers advice and information, advocacy services to connected foster carers across the UK. www.thefosteringnetwork.org.uk.

CHAPTER 2

The Settling Dust?

Overview

Kinship care is a unique and challenging journey for all involved. Most carers liken it to a roller coaster of emotions and can feel drained while navigating a confusing minefield of a system that is supposed to be fair and robust.

Janet's story may be a familiar one. She had never had dealings with Children's Services before and had raised her children to adulthood. While Janet was at work, the police walked in and broke the news to her that her sister had suddenly died. She was told to go to her nephew's school, tell him the tragic news, and take him home. Janet picked up a few of her sister's belongings from the house and her nephew's possessions and locked the door for one last time. She asked the police officer what she must do now, and they said, 'You just have to get on with it'. And that was it: no help, no support and no guidance! She asked the school what she should do, and they said the same. Janet then called Children's Services to ask them for help; they said, 'It's a private arrangement; you need to get PR, go and see a solicitor', and that was it. Janet was devastated that she and her nephew were left alone, struggling with grief.

You can see from Janet's experience that the government, local authorities and professional bodies do lack clear policies and procedures. Each professional body offered its advice based on its level of understanding, leaving the interpretations of rules and guidelines to the local authority, who based their support on resources and finance. No one checked to see if it was okay for Janet to take on her nephew – it was presumed – if they had enough money to live on or had the emotional support to get through this. It is down to if you are fortunate enough to find someone knowledgeable and experienced in their field to guide you.

Janet faced some tough challenges when she became a kinship carer, but things improved when she reached out for help from Citizen's Advice and Kinship Carers UK. With their guidance and support, she was able to overcome those challenges and help her nephew thrive. Now, she's using her experience to assist others in similar situations. Janet's story is a perfect example of the power of seeking help and support when things get tricky.

When walking the kinship road, it is essential not to let a flawed system deter you. Take the time to collect all the relevant information, don't accept that everything you are told is correct, do your research, acquire knowledge, and seek support from various sources. Remember that although life can sometimes be challenging, better days are ahead. Look out for the rainbows (people who help you along the way), and remind yourself that life's storms are temporary.

2A: Why Am I Being Assessed?

[See also 2E: Conflicting Feelings About the Assessment Process, Chapter 8: Working With Others]

Initially there might be a flurry of activity where some emergency checks are done. You might just have an initial police check and a local check with health and social services if a child is moving in very quickly. Once a child has been with you for a few days and the dust has settled, the social workers will be looking at what the best short- or long-term plan is for the child. In order to do this, the regulations say that they need to fulfil certain tick boxes.

When might you be formally assessed?

- If the local authority deems you are 'privately fostering' (for more than 28 days) a connected child. Parental responsibility stays with the child's birth parents, and the child has not been in care or 'looked after'.
- If you are a relative or friend and the local authority or police have placed the child with you due to them not receiving 'suitable care', and the child has been 'in care' or looked after by the local authority.
- Where the court process asks the local authority to prepare a report regarding suitability if special guardianship is being sought.

Often, the local authority will start to formally assess you under the Fostering Regulations. This is when the short- to medium-term plan is for you to become a 'family and friends foster carer' while longer-term plans are made. In this situation, you have to go through the same process as a foster carer, but you are only specifically approved for your connected child or children. Often, kinship carers struggle with this as they tell us they did not want to become a foster carer and have not asked for this. Nevertheless, the majority of local authorities follow the Fostering Regulations closely, although many have tweaked and updated the process to make it more fit for purpose for your unique circumstances.

While it may initially feel ridiculous to assess someone *already caring* for a child, it is important to remember that the assessment process serves a broader purpose. It provides an opportunity to assess your ability to meet the child's *evolving* needs, as well as their current ones. The assessment might be looking far into the future. The process also looks at where additional support or resources may be required.

It might be that the child isn't living with you and is living elsewhere, and the social workers are simultaneously assessing other family or friends.

This can feel really irritating, especially as you may well be related to the child, already have knowledge of them and might have been looking after them perfectly well for long periods of time in the past with nobody at all interfering!

Although it's difficult, try to remember that the social workers do have a job to do, and it is the law that requires them to do it. They may be very sympathetic to your situation, but they still have to tick the boxes.

Some of the areas that the assessment will cover are:

- your relationship with the child
- your health
- your personal history
- your parenting history
- your financial arrangements
- your relationship with partner (if you are part of a couple)
- contact arrangements
- criminal convictions
- your ability to care for the child and to meet their needs now and in the future.

As part of the process, the assessor, or another social worker, will carry out unannounced visits. This can feel very threatening and disconcerting. Remember that child safety is at the forefront of this regulation and no one really enjoys doing these visits! During the visit, they will want to check the child's bedroom and may also check you have enough food in the house. If you feel that you have been unfairly criticized or felt intimidated during an unannounced visit, don't be afraid to speak out, or to contact a support organization to advocate for you (see 1I: Where Can I Go for Help?).

In 2024, at the Centre of Excellence in Child Trauma, in response to many challenges being raised by kinship carers about the assessment process, we devised and piloted the Trauma Informed Parenting Preparation and Assessment for Connected/ Kinship carers (TIPPACK). This process unifies all assessments and also makes sure that kinship carers are given *all* the vital information and training they need. The assessment also includes a Level 1 qualification in trauma-informed parenting. If you would like to know more about this please visit www.inspiretraining-group.com/qualifications.

2B: What Documents Should I Have?

[See also 1D: Essential Things First]

Your documents

There are a few key documents that you need to be aware of and should keep to hand as it's likely you might need to show them lots of times when being assessed! First, think about ID documents. These might be driving licence, passport, utility bills, birth certificates, marriage certificates and that kind of thing.

Child's documents

There are also documents which you should be provided with relating to the child in your care.

You may have 'the red book', especially where a child is under five, as it records all their developmental milestones and has details of health visitors and so on. If you do not have this and have a very young child, you need to ask for it as you will be taking the child for their health check-ups. It's also important to have for young babies, especially if there have been issues with drugs and alcohol in utero, to ensure you have all the information you need to monitor your connected child's health. If ever you have to take the child to the hospital, take this book with you.

You should also be given school information, such as the child's progress, whether or not they have special educational needs and the planning around this, school reports and invitations to parents' evening.

A note about passports

Check who has the child's passport (if there is one), and also their birth certificate. You may need these documents if you are claiming benefits for the child or plan on taking them on holiday. (Note: If the child is subject to a care order or other legal proceedings you normally need permission to take the child out of the local authority.)

It can be a bit of a minefield, getting a passport for your connected child. If they already have a passport, then this is wonderful! A renewal is much more straightforward than applying for a first passport.

Circumstances and requirements vary depending on the legal status of the child. For example, if you are looking after your child under a kinship fostering arrangement, Social Services will still be involved and can assist you in getting all the information you need for the passport. If the child is on a care order, then the social worker will need to give the permission and signature for a passport.

If you now have a Special Guardianship Order then it is down to you to gather all the information you will need for the passport.

At the time of writing (May 2024), it is straightforward to find information on the Government website about applying for a passport where a child is fostered. This is not the case, however, with special guardianship.

As a guide, make sure you have access to/copies of the

following important documents/information which will help you enormously when making a passport application:

- The birth parents' date of birth, place of birth and preferably birth certificates
- Maternal and paternal grandparents' date and place of birth
- Passport numbers of any of the above if applicable.

Frequently, we do not have this information, but we can normally follow one line of the child's birth family. For example, if you are maternal grandparents you will have a lot of the information that you need.

The passport office has an advice line, and this can be very useful. Sometimes the information can vary depending on the knowledge of the person on the other end of the phone! Some people we have spoken to do not understand that special guardians hold parental responsibility.

It's a good idea to contact Kinship Carers UK and the Government website for signposting to up-to-date information about regulations for applying for passports.

The most important thing is to allow yourself a lot of time to make the passport application and be prepared to make your own applications and searches for birth parents' birth certificate and so on.

When you go on holiday, you *must* take a copy of the SGO with you. If you are fostering, you will need a letter of consent from Social Services and possibly the birth parent too. It depends on who holds parental responsibility.

Other essential documents
Court orders: Make sure you get a copy of any orders granted especially ones which give you parental responsibility, such as Special Guardianship orders.

Foster Care Agreement (FCA): The local authority should provide you with the Foster Care Agreement if they have asked you to look after the child under the Fostering Regulations. The FCA outlines all the important matters relating to who does what and when for the child. It tells you things like who has parental responsibility and what your responsibilities are around contact. If you are being assessed under the Fostering Regulations and there are lots of demands being made of you, but you have not been given an FCA, you need to ask for this in writing as soon as possible. Sometimes social workers assume that you have this document when you haven't got it. It does prevent lots of misunderstandings. In our case, it cleared up who could post pictures of the child on social media, for example.

2C: What Are My Rights?

[See also 2H: What if I'm Not Happy?]

As a Kinship Carer, you have certain rights and responsibilities that vary depending on the legal order. This section is designed to equip you with the confidence and knowledge to navigate the process with ease. It's impossible to list all your rights in this book, especially as they will vary depending on what your legal status is in relation to your kinship child. In the meantime, we can provide you with some valuable tips and guidance to help you progress with confidence.

As a kinship carer, it is crucial that you become a strong and confident advocate for your child and yourself in all aspects of their life, just as you would for your biological child. Do not hesitate to speak up and demand the best for your child if you are dissatisfied with any areas, such as their school, contact or meetings, including LAC meetings. Remember, you have the right to take an advocate with you to all meetings, and there are professional children's advocate services available that can support your child and speak on their behalf. Be bold, assertive and confident when advocating for yourself and your child's needs and well-being, and never let anyone dismiss your concerns. For children's advocacy support visit www.barnardos.org.uk and www.nyas.net.

Whatever the kinship order, birth parents retain some parental responsibility (see 1B: Who Is in Charge?), which also means they are financially responsible. Raising a connected child is not something we plan for, especially the financial burden and the complications that it brings with it. You are entitled as a kinship carer to ask birth parents to make a financial contribution towards their child, and you also have a right to apply for child maintenance: www.gov.uk/child-maintenance-service or www.cmsas.com.

Liam and his partner are dedicated, connected foster carers for their five-year-old niece, Tabbitha. Liam discovered that his kinship fostering allowance was below the recommended fostering allowance as stated in the current version of *Family and Friends Care: Statutory Guidance for Local Authorities*. Liam emailed his social worker and asked for a reassessment. Unfortunately, an increase was not awarded, so Liam had no choice but to make a formal complaint, via a form he completed on the local authority website. Again, the request was refused, so Liam finally made his complaint to the Ombudsman for Children's Care Services. Liam was finally awarded not only the amount he was supposed to be paid, but also a reimbursement for the underpayment, which was backdated.

Vicky is a special guardian who has cared for her granddaughter, Lily, for ten years. However, she was struggling to make ends meet with her state pension and universal state benefits. Initially, Vicky was only awarded a small amount of £20 by the local authority, which she thought was all she was entitled to. But, after she requested a financial assessment, the local authority reviewed the situation and increased her allowance to £115.

If you think that your kinship allowance is not enough, it's worth getting in touch with your local authority to enquire about a financial assessment.

If you need a little support or encouragement or want to find out more, please join Kinship Carers UK virtual support groups at www.kinshipcarersuk.com. If you have any concerns with fostering matters, please visit www.thefosteringnetwork.org.uk or https://fosterwiki.com.

2D: What Happens at Court?

[See also 1F: Court Glossary and Who You May See in Court]

Enza Smith writes: Going to court was one of the most terrifying experiences I have ever had. The case lasted a week, and worrying thoughts crossed my mind. What if the local authority and parents changed their minds? However, my biggest fear was that the judge would not award our legal order and my grandchild would end up in the care system.

I walked into the court building slightly early and smartly dressed. I then moved into the security check-in area, which made me feel as if I was going through an airport security checkpoint. I had to empty my bag. The parents, children's legal guardian, social worker and their legal teams walked in separately, and we spent a lot of time waiting around and moving from one room to another while they discussed the case. Finally, after what felt like an eternity, we were called into the courtroom. Before we entered, we were asked to turn off our phones and sit at separate tables, away from one another, with glasses of water in front of us.

The legal teams placed their folders of paperwork on the table and were ready for the hearing. I brought my notepad and an extra pen to write questions for my solicitor. We all had to swear an oath.

Fortunately, I had my legal representative, so she did most of the talking. At one point, the judge did ask the parents and me questions that were not difficult. The case was adjourned as we had not fully agreed on the SGO support plan. We asked for non-means tested allowance and therapeutic support, and getting advice from Kinship Carers UK was the best thing we ever did. (Please see 1I and Chapter 10.) We all returned a day later to have our final discussions. Fortunately, everyone, including the judge, was happy for us to have the legal order, which we received a couple of weeks later.

Important note: You must attend all hearings. You must speak to the court's office if you cannot attend.

Outline of the court process

- **The first hearing:** This is called a directions hearing, where the court decides how an application will proceed. The court sets deadlines for evidence and reports, determines if the child/ren involved should attend future hearings, assesses the use of mediation or other conflict resolution methods, decides if the case should be transferred to a higher court, and schedules the final hearing. The court sends a copy of the order outlining the directions made to you or your solicitor, if you have one.
- **Second hearing:** The court will consider what assessments, statements, reports and evidence should be before the court ahead of any final decision being made. If Social Services believe the child needs to be removed from the parent's care before the final hearing, they will ask the court to grant an Emergency Protection Order or an

Interim Care Order. They will file a document called a care plan setting out where they think the child should live and what contact there should be for each parent and other relevant persons.

- **Issues resolution hearing:** This will take place where matters, including the child's living arrangements and contact, can be agreed on by all parties involved. If an agreement can be reached, there will be no need for a final hearing, and proceedings may end here. Should an agreement not be made, a final hearing will take place.

- **Final hearing:** At this stage, the court will review all reports, statements and evidence presented by all parties involved, including witnesses, before deciding on whether to grant a Special Guardianship Order or Connected Foster Care.

2E: Conflicting Feelings About the Assessment Process

[See also 2A: Why Am I Being Assessed?]

Navigating the assessment process can often be a bewildering and emotionally chaotic experience. Suddenly, you find yourself being evaluated for a role you may have already been fulfilling, causing a mix of conflicting emotions to arise. The additional pressure of having others give their opinions about your suitability can be very challenging, particularly when it involves the child's birth parents (who may well be related to you), or previous partners.

Simultaneously, the involvement of the child's birth parents in the assessment can be a particularly delicate situation, especially when there is a familial connection. The emotions and complexities that sit alongside these relationships may intensify the already challenging assessment process. However, it is crucial to approach this aspect with empathy and an open mind. Remember that whatever the current difficulties are, the birth parents hold a unique perspective and their input can contribute valuable insights into the child's background, needs and experiences.

It might feel really annoying that suddenly you have social workers visiting your house telling you that you have to be assessed! Many people find the whole process very intrusive. Furthermore of course, you may now be very busy looking after a child and dealing with all the difficulties that have arisen since they arrived.

These circumstances present a unique set of challenges that require careful reflection. You will need a level of self-awareness and patience in order to recognize the complex dynamics at play. By trying to think of the bigger picture, we can get through the assessment process and ensure that the well-being of our connected child remains at the centre of our thoughts.

A connected carer who was assessed under the Fostering Regulations said this:

I honestly found the whole thing one of the most challenging things I've ever been through. I couldn't understand why the social workers were literally looking in my kitchen cupboards when I already had my own children who were thriving, attending school and clearly doing really well! It felt like everything was a criticism of me. At the same time, of course, my sister (my connected child's mother) was living the life of Riley and doing whatever she wanted. It was very annoying indeed when the social workers told me they had to ask her opinion about my parenting! It felt like a real slap in the face as she had no idea about how to be a parent. This caused me a lot of anger and put a lot of pressure on our relationship. I also found it annoying that appointments were made and broken very frequently and no one seemed to take into consideration how difficult life was for me. In the end, we went to panel and got through, and it was actually really positive. I was glad I'd been through it in the end, as it really gave me something to feel proud of.

2F: What About School?

You may agree that school has dramatically changed since you left that form of education. Computers may not have been part of the learning process back then, but these days, children are already tech savvy even before they start school! Nevertheless, some things have remained constant, including the ease of communicating with teachers. Whether it's a face-to-face meeting, an email or a call, teachers are always accessible to help kinship children succeed. Therefore, please introduce yourself and tell them as much as you feel necessary about your kinship child.

Starting school can be overwhelming for any child, be it nursery, primary or secondary school, but it can be even more challenging for a kinship child. When choosing a school for your child, here are a few points to look out for:

- Are staff trained in attachment, trauma, adverse childhood experiences (ACEs) and loss?
- Is there a whole-school approach to supporting children with attachment needs?
- How does the school help with transitions?
- What therapeutic support does the school offer children?

Informing your child's teacher about their kinship status is essential. This will help the teacher understand your child's unique needs and work with you to help your child settle in.

There are other benefits to informing your child's teacher

about your situation. You can tell them about your special relationship with the child and whether they like to call you their parent, aunt or grandparent. It's important to remember that occasions like Mother's or Father's Day can be difficult for your child, and they may require some extra support if they don't feel comfortable making a card for their biological parent. By having a conversation with the teacher about this, you can ensure that your child receives all the assistance they need.

Also, it is a good idea to provide the school with a list of authorized people who can collect your child or a password that only authorized individuals know. This will help ensure your child's safety. If you don't want your child's photo to be made public, let the school know and they will respect your wishes.

It's important to know that your child may have priority access to your chosen school due to the legal order and be entitled to extra funding or support in school if they are, or were, 'looked after' or have an SGO. It's worth chatting with the school to see what resources are available to you and your child. Some schools allow the extra funding Pupil Premium Plus to be used for the child's benefit, providing specialist equipment, additional support in school, and support with trips or after-school activities. It's also worth noting that some schools use this funding to access play therapy. The school's designated teacher for 'looked-after' and previously 'looked-after' children can provide information on accessing these resources. You may also have access to a virtual head from the local authority who will help you identify what support your child needs.

Furthermore, if you feel your child is not in the right educational setting, speak to the headteacher and perhaps look for a school more suited to their needs.

The school's team at the Centre of Excellence in Child Trauma have a brilliant book which can really help with signposting and getting the right support in school: *The A–Z of Trauma-Informed Teaching* (Naish *et al.*, 2023).

2G: What Support Can I Get?

[See also 1I: Where Can I Go for Help?, 3E: Professional Help: Supporting Our Children, 7G: Essential Maintenance, Chapter 9: It's Not About the Money, but... and Chapter 10: Making a Plan]

Enza Smith writes: In 1I: Where Can I Go for Help?, we signposted you to different organizations that can be really helpful. But what about immediate, personal support around you?

When we first embarked on our kinship journey with my grandson, my family and friends were incredibly supportive. My family were always there for us, whether it was a phone call or a visit. As my kinship journey developed, I revisited places like play centres and parks. My friends, who were my age with adult children, didn't want to join me. I mean, who could blame them? I tried to meet with them for coffee, but dealing with a traumatized toddler who could not sit still isn't everyone's cup of tea! Gradually, my support network dwindled, my children had moved on with their lives, and my husband passed away. Before I knew it, I was left to navigate this chapter of my life alone.

It wasn't an easy journey, but I managed to adapt and find my path with the help of my fellow kinship carers from Kinship Carers UK. The groups there provided support and consisted of carers from all walks of life with an immeasurable amount of experience and knowledge. Additionally, I made some wonderful new friends at the National Association of Therapeutic Parenting (NATP) Listening Circles. They understood what it's like to parent a child with trauma, and the expertise I encountered was remarkable. I could meet both groups either face to face or virtually, so I did not have to leave home, which was very handy at bedtime!

My journey has taught me to be brave and talk to people like me. So be brave and join a support group online if there is not one near you. You can say as little or as much as you want. They are not doom and gloom or a moan fest; they can sometimes be serious but also fun. It is so important to have like-minded people around who truly understand the challenges we face.

As a connected foster carer, you can access a network of professionals and social workers who can provide various types of support. Some local authorities also offer support groups. However, some carers say it is difficult to talk openly for different reasons and prefer independent support groups. As a kinship carer, you will find that the support available to you is quite different from that of a connected foster carer. It is very dependent on the services the local authority offers.

Kinship Carers UK offers virtual support groups, face-to-face support groups and a virtual Kinship Community Café. They also have a closed Facebook page called Kinship Voices UK, which offers chat facilities for Kinship Carers: www.kinshipcarersuk.com.

For quick and easy access to support you can listen to 'The Therapeutic Parenting Podcast'. There are lots of episodes about all the different topics you may need, including one about where you can go for support. Just ask your smart speaker to play the Therapeutic Parenting Podcast, or visit www.coect.co.uk/podcasts.

Remember that you have the power to take control of your situation and overcome any challenge that comes your way. Regardless of your specific order, you are not alone. There are people to support you and help you become more confident and empowered. Don't hesitate to reach out to them and take charge of your situation. With support, you will be able to move forward with confidence and strength.

2H: What if I'm Not Happy?

[See also 1I: Where Can I Go for Help?, 2C: What Are My Rights?]

There may be occasions during your kinship journey when you find you are not happy with the way things are going. Perhaps there are too many unrealistic demands placed on your family or disagreements with what has been promised.

Lily is a sibling kinship carer. She contacted Kinship Carers UK when a social worker called her to look after her sibling. Lily and her brother Leo were occasionally raised in foster care, and she understood the importance of having a team of professionals around her whom she could call on and trust. We advised Lily to keep a detailed record (timeline) of everything that was said to her and by whom. She needed to ensure that every call and email was cross-referenced, and to note who promised financial help, assistance with getting her brother to school, and even how they would help Lily move to a two-bed-room flat. It soon became clear to her that these were empty promises. Lily invited her support team to the LAC meeting. The social worker denied any of the promises she had made. However, Lily pulled out her file of evidence. The independent reviewing officer immediately called the meeting to an end due to the high tensions in the room.

Lily made a formal complaint through the local authority (LA) website, detailing the broken promises. Within a week, the LA replied. Lily followed the complaint through all the stages, evidencing the detailed diary, emails, texts, calls, dates, times and names, with details of who said what. Lily received the support and finances she was promised. Her brother Leo was given a bus pass and school uniform, and Lily could con-tinue to attend her college course and know there was food in the cupboard to feed her brother and herself. Lily's Member of Parliament and local housing officer helped her get a suitable flat, and some fabulous local charities helped Lily get a bed, carpet and white goods. The last time we heard from Lily, she had completed her studies and started university.

We cannot stress enough about keeping a timeline diary of events and, most importantly, building a professional team around you and your child. Your kinship journey may not be as difficult for you as it was for Lily, but she understood the importance of having a team of friends and professionals around her that she could trust – people to encourage her when she felt alone and out of her depth; people with varied knowledge; people she and Leo could safely confide in and help their voices be heard.

Routes to resolution

- Every local authority will have a complaints procedure which can be accessed online. Don't be afraid to use it!
- You can also contact Ofsted with any complaints or concerns you have about the local authority relating to children's social care. Look on the Government website for up-to-date contact details for your area.
- Ask the Citizens Advice Bureau to help you to identify the best person to complain to.
- Contact the Local Government and Social Care Ombudsman: www.LGO.org.uk.

Who are your trusted friends and professionals?
Think about:

CHAPTER 3

A Different Child?

Overview

Who is this child and why have they changed?

It is a common misconception that children who have experienced trauma and separation should be able to easily adapt to their new surroundings and caregivers. Expectations of the child are often too high, and unrealistic. It is important to accept that your connected child/ren is likely to exhibit changes in behaviour and personality as they try to come to terms with their difficult past experiences.

This can be particularly challenging for those of us who have had a pre-existing relationship with the child. Suddenly, it feels as if we have a different child, with new dynamics at play.

Instead of trying to force the child to fit into the previous 'relationship mould', we must adapt to the child's needs and emotions. By doing so, we can create a safe and supportive environment for our child to heal and grow.

Understanding the complexity of trauma and its effects on children is essential in order to provide the necessary support and care. Our approach to the unfolding situation must be with empathy, patience and an open mind. Every child's experience is unique but will always require a trauma-informed (or therapeutic parenting) approach.

By acknowledging the changes that occur in children who have experienced trauma, we can better equip ourselves to provide the love, understanding and support that they so desperately need. It is through this understanding and adaptation that we can help our children find their way back to a sense of security and confidence.

3A: The Child's Perspective

[See also Chapter 4: Therapeutic Parenting [Trauma-Informed Parenting]]

Kinship carers, foster parents and adopters often face a challenging situation when the child they are caring for maintains a strong loyalty and protectiveness towards their birth parents, even after experiencing abuse. It can be difficult to comprehend and accept this behaviour, especially when it seems to put the child in danger or goes against everyone's better judgement.

It is crucial to understand that these attachments are often formed out of fear. The child may feel a deep need to make their parent love them, especially if they feel unloved, and this drives them to seek out that love, even if it is not in their best interest. We must approach these circumstances with patience, understanding and a therapeutic mindset.

Instead of vilifying or speaking negatively about the birth parents, we must maintain honesty and open communication with the child. This allows the child to feel safe and secure in sharing their concerns with us, knowing that they will be listened to and supported.

Overcoming these often heartbreaking issues takes time and a deep level of empathy from kinship carers. By adopting an empathic approach with kindness, nurture and a focus on the child's well-being, it is possible to help them navigate their feelings and rebuild attachments in a healthy way.

The conflicting feelings which arise for us, however, can be difficult to deal with. We may feel very torn about the relationship the child has with their birth parent, especially if our relationship with the parent is a close one. Alternatively, where there is a fracture in the relationship, it can be tempting to speak negatively about the birth parents in order to protect the child. This almost always backfires!

With very young children, they will have little or no understanding about what has happened. All they will know is that someone who was there every day suddenly isn't. We might see the child moving through stages of grief, fear, anger, hopelessness and rejection.

Throughout all of this, we must remain the 'unassailable safe base', helping the child with strong routines, consistency, reliability and predictability.

3B: Developmental Trauma

[See also 3D: Diagnoses, 4E: Teaching Cause and Effect]

Developmental trauma is a complex and often misunderstood condition that has its roots in early childhood experiences. It can be difficult to accept that a child who has been removed at birth may suffer from developmental trauma, but it's important to recognize the impact of what happened in utero, as well as after the child was born.

During pregnancy, a child is incredibly sensitive to the environment around them. Exposure to stress, violence and substance and alcohol abuse can have a profound impact on their developing brain and nervous system. This can lead to long-term effects on their ability to regulate emotions, link cause and effect, form healthy relationships, and understand the world around them.

One of the key factors in developmental trauma is unmet need. When a child's basic needs for safety, security and love are not met (or met sporadically and unreliably), it can lead to a sense of fear partnered with a constant need to seek out safety. For example, if a child was left alone for long periods of time, the underlying fear is one of being forgotten about, or being left to go hungry. The behaviours that partner up with this are what some might call 'attention-seeking behaviours'. Actually, they are 'attachment-seeking behaviours' as the child is driven by fear to keep your focus on them.

As therapeutic (or trauma-informed) parents, it is our responsibility to help these children feel safe and secure, and to understand the root of their behaviours. We explain a lot about this and how we do it in Chapter 4.

It's important to recognize that the effects of developmental trauma may not be immediately obvious, but they can become so later in life. Sometimes, therapeutic parents can be a bit overly optimistic in the early years, believing there are no effects of developmental trauma, only to find that this surfaces as the child grows.

3C: A Different Parent

[See also 11E: Who Am I Now?]

Enza Smith writes: I got a call from Children's Services: either take your grandchild, or he will be adopted! Wow, I was in shock. Baby Bradley was brought to me with empty, staring open eyes and not making a sound. I rolled up my sleeves: 'I've done this once before, so I can do it again.' I showered this baby boy with love and attention and treated him as my own.

My grandson became my top priority. It was surprising how quickly we bonded. Even though I was his nan, I was like his mum and did everything a loving mother would do for him. Our bond grew stronger every day. Despite knowing I was his nan, Bradley asked if he could call me Mum. He just wanted to be like his friends who had mums. We hadn't seen Bradley's mum for five years until she suddenly wanted to meet him. We arranged to meet in a garden centre café with a play area, somewhere public. It felt strange to see my daughter again after so long, and though I still had love for her, things were not the same any more.

In Bradley's eyes, my daughter was not his mother. He saw her as a lady who played with him and told him she was his mum. Although Bradley accepted this as a given name, he would often come to me for reassurance and say, 'You are my real mum, aren't you, Nanny?' This made my daughter feel instantly rejected, not just by her son but by me, too. She didn't like her son seeing me as his mum. At that point, I realized our family dynamics would never be the same again.

For some carers, it is often challenging to navigate divided loyalties. Being caught in the middle and having to 'choose a side' can be painful for everyone involved, especially the child. It can be challenging to balance your love and desire to protect your child with your child's best interests. Choosing sides may also result in managing your child's or other family member's anger towards you, contributing to feelings of guilt and anger. This can create a vicious cycle that adds to the already difficult situation.

You may wonder what to do next.

- **The child comes first.** Make it clear to everyone involved that the child's best interests come first.
- **Ditch the self-blame.** You have demonstrated that your love and commitment to your child is paramount. It's important to remember that this situation is not your fault.

- **Bring in a professional or a neutral friend.** If you feel you cannot meet together alone with the birth parents, find a mediator to help you all explain roles.
- **Set firm rules.** Work some essential boundaries and rules out with the child's parent.
- **Keep it positive.** Don't say negative things about the child's parents, especially to the child.
- **Keep the child out of the middle.** Don't force the child to take sides between you and their parents. Remember that if divided loyalties are painful for you, they are more so for the child.
- **Get support.** Talk to your family or look for a support group in person or online; it can help you to talk to other carers.

3D: Diagnoses

[See also 1I: Where Can I Go for Help?, 3B: Developmental Trauma, 3E: Professional Help: Supporting Our Children]

Your connected child may come to you with lots of different diagnoses and it can be really worrying and conflicting trying to find your way through all these. Unfortunately, sometimes our children are misdiagnosed or remain undiagnosed. We must accept that if a child has suffered trauma they *will* be suffering from developmental trauma.

Developmental trauma often masquerades as different conditions because of the resulting behaviours and coping strategies arising from the way the brain has formed.

Common diagnoses for children who have suffered trauma include:

- Attention deficit hyperactivity disorder (ADHD)
- Sensory processing disorder
- Autism
- Oppositional defiance disorder
- Dyspraxia or developmental coordination disorder
- Global developmental delay.

Sarah Naish writes: At the Centre of Excellence in Child Trauma, we say that these can often seem like *symptoms* of developmental trauma. So it's a bit like having the symptoms of a cold and the doctor gives you paracetamol but you actually have pneumonia – the doctor is just treating a symptom and not the underlying cause.

There are of course standalone diagnoses that are absolutely valid and accurate of autism or ADHD. It's just that if your child has high cortisol levels due to having suffered trauma, it's practically impossible to tell the difference between that and ADHD! A diagnosis of ADHD or autism can be very helpful in school because the teachers then know how to respond and react to a child. So even if that turns out to be a misdiagnosis, it can still be helpful.

Frequently, parents of children from trauma tell us that they knew their child was really struggling but they couldn't get a diagnosis. The important thing here is to see what the impact is on the child and on the family, and to deal with it as we go along. As the effects of trauma reduce, we may well see a different child.

I learned that my children's diagnoses were incorrect as they became older and 'grew out of' these conditions. These are conditions you don't grow out of, like autism for example. However, while they were growing up, it did feel and look like that.

Keep an open mind and if you feel your child needs a diagnosis, then by all means push for that and keep pushing. See our useful support organizations in Chapter 1 for help with this.

3E: Professional Help: Supporting Our Children

[See also 2G: What Support Can I Get?]

Life is a journey that can be filled with both good and bad times. There are moments of joy when everything seems to be going well, moments of sorrow, such as when we lose someone close to us, and moments of difficulty when we struggle with the trauma of our child's past and the fact that we can see they are suffering too. Sometimes, we may feel overwhelmed by the challenges that life throws, but it's important to remember that you are not alone. In 2G we looked at support for us as adults; here, we are looking at support services for children.

If you are a connected carer who is fostering, you can speak with your social worker, who can guide you towards the local services for the child. However, if you find this difficult or you are a kinship carer, irrespective of your legal order, you can contact your Early Help team within your local authority.

Other professional services for children

Adoption and Special Guardianship Support Fund (ASF): This is currently available to children up to 21 and adults up to 25 with an Education, Health and Care plan in England. If your child was previously looked after before the child had a CAO or SGO, you can access services for therapy and specialist assessment through your local authority.

Bereavement: You may be able to access services from your local hospice or contact other charities, such as Winston's Wish, which offers bereavement support and counselling for children. They also help adults who are caring for young grieving people. www. winstonswish.org.

CAMHS: This is a free NHS service that helps children and young people with emotional, behavioural and mental health difficulties. Their teams include psychiatrists, psychologists, therapists, nurses, social workers and other professionals specializing in working with children and families. A child's GP usually makes the referral, but it can also come from a school or health visitor. They work with children and young people up to the age of 25.

Mental health: Young Minds has a great website. They offer support, guidance and advice to children, and also information and guidance on getting help, such as early help and intervention, counselling and therapy, how to get help from your GP and a guide to CAMHS: www.youngminds.org.uk. The helpline number is 0808 802 5544.

Special Educational Needs and Disabilities Information Advice and Support Service (SENDIASS): Free and impartial information, advice and support for the families of children and young people with disabilities or special education needs: www. kids.org.uk/sendiass-home.

There are also some really helpful therapeutic parenting children's books which can connect children to the feelings they have and help them to understand their own behaviours. For example, the therapeutic parenting children's books series by Sarah Naish (Jessica Kingsley Publishers), such as *William Wobbly and the Very Bad Day* (2016).

CHAPTER 4

Therapeutic Parenting (Trauma-Informed Parenting)

Overview

Sarah Naish writes: In training, I often talk about the difference between penguins and birds. This is relevant when we think about our children who have developmental trauma and often a different way of thinking. Just because a penguin has wings, it doesn't mean it can fly. Just because our children smile and look as if they understand what's going on, it doesn't mean that they're able to do all that we think they should.

We have to be very careful that we are adapting the child's world in order that they can feel safe, so they can grow and form secure attachments. We can only do this by adopting a trauma-informed (or therapeutic parenting) approach. You can read all about this in *The A–Z of Therapeutic Parenting* (Naish, 2018), but in this chapter we will cover some of the most important points for you.

4A: Emerging Behaviours: Why Our Children Need Therapeutic Parenting

[See also 3D: Diagnoses]

What behaviours might we expect to see from our children where they have suffered trauma? Well, first of all we have to think about unmet needs. Many children who come into care do so because they have not had their needs met. This is explained more in 4C: Identifying the Child's Unmet Needs.

The difficulty is that when a child's survival needs are left unmet because the parent is unavailable physically and/or emotionally, or fails to feed them regularly, the child's brain begins to develop differently. They become very focused on their own survival. Attachment therapist Sarah Dillon says, 'An unmet need remains unmet until it is met.' Most of the behaviours you will see in children from trauma are simply the child trying to get their needs met.

When we think about a child who has not had regular food, there is an unmet need there around needing to make sure they've got a secure food supply. When a child has not been tended to in the night, they may be very difficult to settle. In this way, the child is communicating their inner distress through their behaviour.

Our children may also have been extremely frightened and some of their actions will arise from fear. It's common to see the following specific behaviours as a result of these feelings:

- Controlling behaviours
- Rejection
- Hypervigilance
- Aggression
- Anger

- Running away
- Hiding
- Nonsense chatter (excessive)
- Lying (excessive)
- Stealing (excessive)
- Sibling rivalry (intense).

We must also remember to notice the child who is quiet, withdrawn and overly compliant. These children can easily be overlooked but they have learned to internalize their grief, sadness and fear and it can be much more difficult to reach them as they grow older. Always be alert for the child who is very willing to please and pretending that they are 'just like you'. This is a survival strategy that has kept the child safe in the past. In the same way, they may continue to over-identify with an absent, dangerous parent in the mistaken belief or fear that the parent may return.

High cortisol is a real 'behaviour highlight' for our children because in the past, cortisol would have been a major factor in keeping them alert and driving their survival behaviours. Cortisol does not diminish very quickly and it means that our children are in a constant state of high alert and 'busyness'. Quick to react and slow to calm. We may notice that they are easily distracted, driven to eat sugary snacks (however they can get them) and are always 'on the go'.

It can be very tempting to oversimplify these behaviours and just decide that a child is 'being naughty' and that standard parenting will 'soon sort it out'. That is simply not the case. Our children are frightened, and their behaviours will continue to spiral unless we can give them the reassurance they need through therapeutic parenting.

4B: What Is Therapeutic [Trauma-Informed] Parenting?

It may be useful to start off with an explanation about the terms 'therapeutic parenting' and 'trauma-informed parenting'. Trauma-informed parenting or therapeutic parenting are the *same style of parenting* and are interchangeable terms that are commonly used for people who are looking after children who have suffered some kind of trauma, as a result of early life neglect and/or abuse or from other traumatic events. The only difference is where a parent has a neurotypical child who has not suffered any form of abuse. They are likely to refer to their parenting style as 'therapeutic parenting' rather than 'trauma-informed parenting'.

As the majority of readers of this book may well be caring for children who have experienced trauma then we will continue to use the term 'therapeutic parenting'.

Therapeutic parenting is a different way of life. Parents need to *live* as therapeutic parents with their connected children. It is not something we can choose to dip in and out of. The therapeutic parent will live a life that is well structured with strict routines and boundaries. Where a child has suffered trauma, there is no emotional room for surprises, spontaneous outings or uncertainty. Therapeutic parenting is also very effective for securely attached children, so there does not need to be any conflict in parenting style if you also have securely attached or neurotypical children alongside children who have experienced trauma.

The aim of therapeutic parenting is to enable a traumatized child to recover from the trauma that they have experienced. With a neurodiverse child, who may have sensory issues or find it difficult to self-regulate (calm themselves), the aim is to help the child to live in a world which can seem overwhelming and frightening to them.

Therapeutic parents achieve this by developing new pathways in the child's brain to help them to link cause and effect, reduce their levels of fear and shame, and to support them to start to make sense of their world.

Therapeutic parenting mainly differs from other parenting styles because it has an *enhanced level of therapeutic responses and empathy* within the parenting style. We might be more familiar with standard 'good parenting' techniques (time out, reward charts etc.) advocated by some social work and health professionals, but be assured that therapeutic parenting is the only way forward for re-parenting a child with developmental trauma.

Looking from the outside in, therapeutic parenting may sometimes appear 'strict' or 'rigid'. The reason for this is that our children really need more structure than is provided by standard parenting. Therapeutic parents will also allow the child to experience 'natural consequences' in order to help them to link cause and effect and to learn about their impact on the world. We explain this more later in this section.

Useful resources

What Is Therapeutic Parenting? YouTube: www.tinyurl.com/4x56sk9a.

Understanding Your Traumatised Child. YouTube: www./tinyurl.com/3uxkbvfm.

4C: Identifying the Child's Unmet Needs

Sarah Naish writes: In 4A: Emerging Behaviours: Why Our Children Need Therapeutic Parenting, it was explained that the most challenging behaviours we see arise from unmet need. We must think about what our child's unmet needs might be. Any child who has experienced trauma or inconsistent care will have unmet needs. We often mention 'the seed of unmet need' because therapeutic parents need to find that seed and water it in order for our children to grow into healthy, securely attached individuals. Our children are really good at telling us what they need *through their behaviours*. Unfortunately, this can be misinterpreted.

It's all too easy to think about tricky behaviours as 'naughty' or 'attention seeking' rather than expressing an unmet need. Let's stop and think for a moment – why might a child need attention? Maybe because that was something they lacked in their formative years. It's not attention seeking; it's *attachment seeking*, and attachment is essential for healthy emotional growth.

We have to put our detective hats on a bit and work out what the behaviour of our children is telling us. It's useful to remember the acronym AIR:

- Accept there are unmet needs.
- Identify what they are.
- Respond to that unmet need.

The first thing we need to do is accept that our children *have* unmet needs. This may not be an easy thing for kinship carers to do, because if we accept that our children have needs that were not met, this means that someone (who perhaps we love or are close to) failed to meet that child's needs. This can be a very painful truth to accept.

Once we have accepted that our child's behaviours are telling us there is an unmet need, we need to look at the behaviours to help us *identify* what that unmet need is. For example, if a child is waking a lot in the night and demanding attention and drinks, it's useful to think about what *age* you would have expected to have seen that behaviour from a child. Perhaps a very young baby. So, if this child was not seen to in the night, if they didn't get a drink of milk when they needed it, if they weren't comforted or reassured, that need remains unmet. The child is going to continue to wake in the night until we go and meet the need that wasn't met in their first few months of life. We meet that need through our response.

There are so many ways we can respond to children to help fill all those gaps, and to meet their unmet needs. That is what therapeutic parenting is all about. We explain more about this in the next section.

4D: Bridging the Gap – Meeting the Unmet Need

Sarah Naish writes: One of the ways that we meet unmet needs is by responding to what the child's behaviour is *telling us*, rather than reacting to what the behaviour *is*. I did this with my children using empathic commentary and 'naming the need'. There is a difference between the two as 'empathic commentary' is used very much in the moment and 'naming the need' tends to go back to the early life experience of the child. You can read much more about this with related strategies for any behaviour in my book *The A–Z of Therapeutic Parenting*. At the Centre of Excellence in Child Trauma, we also have lots of webinars on this topic, and free podcasts.

Empathic commentary example

The child is not getting ready for school and is hiding. Instead of saying, 'Stop being naughty and come and get your shoes on!', I might say, 'I can see you're feeling a bit wobbly about school today. I wonder if that's why you are hiding?'

The underlying factor here is anxiety. Perhaps the child is struggling to deal with transitions because change can be scary. There also might be things going on at school that make the child feel very unsafe. So, when we respond in this way using empathic commentary we are also identifying that unmet need of parental presence and reassurance. This could also relate to those early days when the baby *should* have had their needs anticipated and met by the parent.

Naming the need example

The child is stealing lots of high sugar items. You have tried everything you can to resolve this but have had no success. You've done all the standard parenting stuff, like explaining they'll 'get fat', or 'all their teeth will fall out', and so on, but nothing seems to work.

In this scenario, I said to my daughter, 'I've noticed that you often take lots of chocolate when you have been on your own. I think "little Emily" was left alone a lot and was very frightened and hungry. Now you're "big Emily", little Emily still really needs you to find lots of sugar to fill that big empty space of fear and worry inside you. The difficulty is that no matter how much chocolate you eat, it's not going to fill that big empty space inside. That space was made because you didn't have enough cuddles, hugs and people looking after you when you were very little.'

Although this didn't make a miraculous change immediately, my daughter explained that when she went to take the chocolate next time it was as if she could hear my voice telling her why she was doing it. Over time, this meant that her self-esteem grew, and the behaviour stopped. It also meant we could reference this when it happened subsequently. This is a much more positive dialogue than, 'I can't believe you stole AGAIN!'

When we ask a child why they did something, the child hears, 'I am bad'. It's our job to remove this toxic shame and give the child a more positive view of themselves. Using these strategies which identify and explain unmet needs to the child gives the child a much more positive narrative.

If you are worried about guessing wrong, or are a bit unsure about using these statements, you can use my therapeutic parenting children's stories; for example, *Rosie Rudey and the Enormous Chocolate Mountain* (Naish, 2018) has the mum using naming the need about this exact issue in the story. You can read the story to your child and see what they say!

4E: Teaching Cause and Effect

We need to remember that perhaps the child's actions when they were younger made little impact on the world. For example, if they were hungry, maybe they stayed hungry? If they cried, perhaps nobody came? For this reason, our children are very impulsive and need everything *now*. They can't link cause and effect when we say that there will be a consequence for their behaviour next Tuesday, for something they did today!

We can help our children to understand their own behaviours by using 'natural consequences' and 'logical consequences'.

With *natural consequences*, we are helping the child to learn about their impact on the world by allowing events to take their natural course.

With *logical consequences*, we intervene by putting in a consequence that is closely linked to the child's action. This helps the child to link 'I did that, so this happened'.

It is *very* important that we remember to add in nurture to whatever the consequences are, otherwise the relationship can be damaged and the child may withdraw or escalate behaviours.

Here are some examples of what this looks like.

Natural consequences

Event	Natural consequence	Nurture
Child breaks phone	Phone is broken, child has no phone.	Empathize about how sad it is the phone was broken. Offer to help make a savings plan.
Child lies down on ground on the way to school refusing to move	Child is late for school.	Provide parental presence – wait with child.

Child is unkind to their friend	Friend rejects child.	Give support around sadness child feels about loss of relationship.

Logical consequences

Event	Logical consequence	Nurture
Child hits sibling on the arm	Time needs to be spent putting cream on sibling's arm to help them 'feel better',	Can be done together with reflection about how you know the child has 'a good heart'.
Child damages car	It isn't safe to take the child out in the car for the day. Lots of walking!	Empathy around wanting to make sure the child is safe.
Child makes hole in their door	Child is helped to do the repair themselves. It may take a while and another more fun activity can be sacrificed.	Offer to help and give low-key praise on the repair, whatever it looks like!

By giving our children this gift of understanding the impact of their actions, we give them the gift of a more positive future.

4F: Awareness of Change

Sarah Naish writes: Sometimes when I am training, kinship carers will come up to me and say they're really pleased that the child they're looking after doesn't seem to have any issues. They might even go on to tell me that the child was removed at birth and therefore they're not anticipating any problems.

Now, they might be one of the lucky ones, and if that is indeed the case, I am thrilled for them. However, years later the same people often come up to me and say, 'You know I told you six years ago that I had no issues with my granddaughter? Well, it's all different now. We don't know what to do for the best.'

After a brief discussion, I can sometimes pinpoint difficulties that occurred during pregnancy. Often there were also difficulties just shortly after the birth or during the birth. There was also, of course, the primal separation from the birth parent, which can cause attachment difficulties.

Even when everything feels absolutely fine, and we really believe that all will be okay, it's still important that we keep an eye out for any changes which might happen. I had ten clear years with my son where everything was absolutely great, and then suddenly at the age of 13 we hit a bit of a brick wall.

Don't start panicking that you've got all the parenting wrong. If you're doing your best with therapeutic parenting, then you're doing the right thing. At some point our children's trauma *has* to come out. It doesn't matter whether that is prenatal trauma, early life, birth trauma or developmental trauma from neglect, abuse or drug/alcohol abuse. Those behaviours will surface so that the child can tell you what they need.

Try not to be afraid of these changes but meet them head on. You can get all the help you need about emerging behaviours in *The A–Z of Therapeutic Parenting* (Naish, 2018).

4G: Emotional Stage vs Chronological Age

[See also 3B: Developmental Trauma, 3D: Diagnoses,
4C: Identifying the Child's Unmet Needs]

One of the best ways we can help our children to catch up lost developmental milestones is to think about what their behaviour is telling us.

As I mentioned in 4C: Identifying the Child's Unmet Needs, if we had a six-month-old baby who was crying at night we wouldn't go in and tell them to stop being silly, reminding them they would be tired in the morning. We would respond to that child because that behaviour in that age child tells us that they are fearful, hungry, in pain, need changing or something else is wrong.

When children miss out stages and early nurture, they also miss out on stages of development. When you are struggling with your child's behaviour and you're feeling as if they're acting immaturely, ask yourself:

- At what age would I normally expect a child to be behaving in this way?
- What would I do in normal circumstances for a child of that age who was behaving that way?

In this way, not only are we identifying unmet needs, but we are responding to the child at the *emotional stage* they are at rather than holding onto expectations about their chronological age.

There is nothing more irritating than going to school with the child and the school saying, 'He's eight so now he *should* be doing XYZ.' I used to reply, 'Well, that would be great of course if he had had everything he needed in his early life. Unfortunately, my child's brain isn't functioning the same way as a child of eight, so he has learning and extra support needs.'

Just because we cannot *see* the problems, it does not mean they are not there!

CHAPTER 5

Family Tensions, Visits and Family Time (Contact)

Overview

Family time or 'planned visiting', often referred to as 'contact', provides birth parents, separated siblings and other extended family members with an environment in which they can interact. The interaction can occur either in a contact centre under supervision, in the community with a trusted adult, or unsupervised if it is safe for the child. The arrangements for visits may depend on the type of contact arrangement made by the local authority or directed by the courts, including leaving it to the carers to arrange. It can take different forms, such as face to face, phone, virtual or postal/email.

Family time can be one of the most challenging experiences for many kinship carers. It can go smoothly if everyone accepts and adheres to the rules and boundaries. Otherwise, this process can turn to resentment. One of the factors that makes planned visits difficult during this time is the family dynamics, which undergo significant changes, including the changing of the carer's role from perhaps aunt to mother or uncle to father or grandparent to parent; this can be a struggle, especially for some birth parents.

If you have been a foster carer and have been looking after a child for some time, then it is likely that contact arrangements will already be in place. They may be reviewed when and if an SGO is granted due to the change in parental responsibility.

Tina's daughter had three children by two fathers; the birth fathers Tina thought were out of the picture as she had not seen them at home with the children. She had a good relationship with her daughter and was happy to be a grandparent and help when needed. Tina explained:

> I naturally fell into the hierarchical role within our family. It was great at the start, and I loved being a grandmother, working, doing my hobbies, going on holidays and spending quality time with my grandchildren. However, due to domestic abuse, the children were removed and placed with me under an Interim Care Order. Then, sadly, just like that, our family dynamics changed once the children came to live with me. It quickly became strained, starting with supervising visits as I was told I had to do this as a connected foster carer. It was the most awkward and challenging time I had ever experienced, especially with the birth fathers, whom I had no relationship with and who had moved their resentment with the local authority onto me. Family life was never the same once our kinship journey started. The birth fathers did not want to be told what they could or could not do with their children, and my relationship with my daughter was at breaking point. I was often told, 'They are my children. You can't tell me what to do!' It took us all a long time to adjust.

The change in family dynamics can cause parents to feel resentful as they adjust to their new life. It is essential to understand and acknowledge the challenges of changing roles during the kinship care journey and make family time safe and comfortable for the children as everyone adjusts to the new normal.

As a connected foster carer, you may find it challenging when the local authority intervenes in your family's day-to-day life. They may have idealistic views of what is normal, which may not align with your family's unique situation. However, as the child's carer, it is your responsibility to make decisions that are in the child's best interests, even if they are difficult. Remember, circumstances and times change, and what works for your family now may not work in the future. Therefore, it is essential to keep an open mind and be prepared to make tough decisions when necessary.

5A: Changing Relationships

Sarah Naish writes: When we are looking after children who have visits with their birth parents or other extended family members, there can be tension and stress in our 'other' family life.

In my own family, I became the person who was supervising the visits with my grandson's birth mother, one of my daughters. I suddenly found that I was in an interesting position of making sure that I allayed my older daughter's (his kinship carer) fears about him going off for visits with me to birth mum, her sister. After all, she had full-time care of him. I needed to do this while reassuring his birth mother that she had a valuable part to play in her son's life.

This is a tricky balancing act because kinship carers are often the ones who are supervising visits with birth family, but they also have a pre-existing relationship. It can be very difficult to preserve your relationship with the child's birth parents if they are angry with you or blame you in some way for what has happened with their child.

I found it helpful to keep everything very factual and practical.

I explained to my daughters that it was essential for us to communicate honestly, openly and preferably in writing, so there could be no misunderstandings about dates, times, location or expectations around equipment and so on.

It doesn't mean that you have to stop being the parent of your adult child if that's the circumstances you're in. I would make other times to spend with my younger daughter, away from visits, and also communicate with her by telephone to ensure she had support and access to her mum. I'm not saying this wasn't a difficult balancing act, it was, but when you hold what is best for the *child* in mind and think about what their life and relationships are going to be like in the future, it becomes easier.

It can be too tempting to put the future to one side and only concentrate on the here and now. This is not a sensible idea. Children grow up faster than we plan for and then they will be able to vote with their feet about who they have relationships with. It's our job to make sure they have realistic expectations, and understanding of the whole extended family.

5B: Blame and Judgement

(See also 2G: What Support Can I Get?, 6C: Dealing With Input From Others (Child's Story)

Enza Smith writes: Regardless of how a kinship child comes to live with you, every kinship carer will feel judged or even blamed at some point on their kinship journey. This could be by professionals, birth parents, family members, friends or even strangers at the local supermarket who observe your kin child having a meltdown as you walk through the door.

In my case, my grandson had abundant energy and often had difficulties controlling himself. He was the boy who couldn't sit still for love nor money. He climbed all over the play equipment instead of playing on it and ran around as if competing with Usain Bolt. I have encountered my fair share of tutting, eye-rolling and muttering. It hurt, but I refused to let it get to me. I have been judged and blamed throughout my kinship journey for many things.

Then judgements came from professionals, who asked questions such as, 'Where did it go wrong as a parent?' and 'How are things going at home as your grandson is all over the place, he will not communicate?' Then others suggested that because he was not my own child, I was being too lenient and spoiling him. Surely I wouldn't have let my own children behave like that? I could go on.

Then comes self-scrutiny. Was it me? Could I have done better? And then comes the self-blame, if only... And while you are licking your self-inflicted wounds, the very people whom you have helped by changing the whole course of your life, caring for and loving their child, leave your life, and it never changes back to what it once was. I learned to recognize the difference between healthy personal responsibility and unhealthy self-blame. It was crucial for my well-being, as I realized that not everything was or is my fault. Yes, I have made mistakes and needed to accept them, as no one is perfect. If you face unfair judgement or blame, don't let it get you down. You can take control of the situation and come out on top. Be confident in yourself and your abilities; don't be afraid to speak up and share your thoughts and feelings.

Remember that keeping things to yourself can be isolating and unproductive. Instead, join a support group or seek out a trusted friend who can help you gain a fresh perspective and find a solution. With confidence and determination, you can overcome any obstacle and emerge stronger.

The A–Z of Survival Strategies: From Chaos to Cake (Naish, 2022) provides lots of strategies for dealing with blame and judgement and how to build your resilience.

5C: Difficulties With Visits (Contact) With Birth Parents

Communication between kinship carers and birth parents can be challenging due to various reasons, such as disagreements over family time rules and boundaries, our beliefs, opinions and the harm our connected children have experienced at the hands of their birth parents. Conflict can also arise from differences in personalities, perspectives and communication styles, and generation gaps.

Additionally, past unresolved issues and emotional situations surrounding the removal of a kinship child can also contribute to family conflicts. Therefore, as legal guardians of the children, we have to prioritize their well-being and agree to court orders, even if it means we have to make decisions that do not align with our views, opinions or beliefs. But this has to work both ways; birth parents also have to comply with the rules set and put the welfare of their children above their wishes and feelings.

Planned visits vary from family to family, and with all families, conflicts arise for various reasons, so it is essential to try and resolve them calmly and quickly.

When things go wrong

Some birth parents may find it challenging to spend quality time with their children and may exhibit unacceptable behaviours or attend under the influence of drugs or alcohol. It's important to remember that you and your kinship child *do not* have to tolerate abusive, controlling, aggressive or unacceptable behaviour. If this is the case, calmly end the visit immediately, or if you feel you are in immediate danger, call the police and take your kinship child to a safe place.

If you are a connected carer, it's essential to immediately contact your social worker and the child's social worker about the situation. Keep a detailed record of all incidents and request that family time be supervised in a contact centre. Your social worker can also talk to the birth parents or other party and explain how their behaviour is unacceptable and not in the child's best interest.

- It is also helpful to keep a detailed diary of the behaviours that you experienced, including the date, time and location, witnesses, if any, and police incident number if they were called.
- You can write an email to the birth parent explaining which aspects of their behaviour were unacceptable during contact and that this type of behaviour must not be repeated.
- You can also suggest alternative forms of contact that you feel are acceptable, such as the supervision of contact by another family member or meeting in a different public space.
- If you feel that contact is too challenging to manage independently, and the other suggestions have not worked, you can suggest a contact centre as an alternative.

If you cannot resolve the situation amicably you can apply to the court to change the contact order, which may involve a family group conference, to help resolve the issues. Contact orders are not written in stone; either party can change them, increase or reduce them if it is in the child's best interest.

5D: Family Time and Visits (Contact): Setting Boundaries

Sam is a kinship carer for her cousin Millie, who is two years old and under an SGO. Family time was arranged by the court for every other week, for two hours out in the community, which Sam would supervise. The court ordered Sam to organize the family time at a suitable time and location for her and Millie. Millie's birth mother wanted to meet at the local town and wander around the shops, so Sam agreed so as not to upset the family. However, Millie didn't enjoy sitting in a pushchair for two hours and cried most of the time.

In response, Sam suggested meeting at the local soft play centre, where Millie could spend quality time playing with her birth mother. This was in the same area, so it was not inconvenient for the birth mother. At first, everything was working well, but then the birth mum started missing quite a few contacts and complained that it was boring. Sam suggested they meet up once a month, but the birth mum became abusive and angry, demanding that she be in charge of family time because Millie was her daughter. Sam relented, and things continued to get worse.

That's when Sam contacted Kinship Carers UK, who provided solutions that would suit her and Millie. She then sent an email to the birth mum setting clear boundaries and expectations. It was challenging at first, but after a while, they established a mutually agreeable relationship that worked for everyone.

Agreed boundaries are essential and establish what one person will accept from another person in actions, behaviours and words. Boundaries are created to keep out negative behaviours such as manipulation, harassment, cruelty and abuse and encourage positive behaviours instead. Boundaries are necessary for promoting healthy relationships, as you could be in communication with birth parents until your kinship child is 18 or beyond.

It's always a good idea to establish clear and acceptable boundaries with birth parents, regardless of the quality of your relationship with them. This can make it easier for you to manage contact now and in the future, should things change.

If you haven't planned family time or feel things have gone in an undesirable direction, it's essential to start by setting clear boundaries. If you have a problematic relationship with the birth parents, you must ensure that your child does not witness this.

- Communicate your boundaries clearly, respectfully and non-confrontationally; try using email or text. This will also eliminate any confusion about what was discussed.
- Know your limits; this will help you support realistic boundaries that you can stick to.
- Don't be afraid to say no. It's okay to say no if their requests or expectations are unreasonable or they do not respect your boundaries.
- Seek support. If you are having difficulty setting boundaries with birth parents, consider seeking support from Kinship Carers UK, a trusted friend or a family member.
- Practise self-care. Take care of yourself and prioritize your needs and well-being. This can help you feel more confident and assertive in setting boundaries.
- Take a break from your relationship with the birth parents and ask a family or friend to help.

5E: Family Time/Planned Visits (Contact): How Much Is Too Much?

How much is too much?

Unfortunately, there is no one-size-fits-all answer to this question. You can and must have a say in this answer, as you and your kinship child have the right to a well-balanced home life and should not be pushed into unrealistic expectations.

Everybody's kinship journey is different depending on various factors, such as why the child was removed or living with you, the child's age, if the child wants to see their birth parents, the social worker's perspective, the court's view on contact, where you live in the country, and so much more. But everyone needs to remember that it has to be in the child's best interests and acceptable. It has to be at the child's pace, especially if they need time to adjust and recover from their ordeal.

In the early stages, while the courts are determining if the child is to be removed or to live with you, birth parents can have weekly multiple family time sessions, which may put a strain on your own family and work-life balance. If you find that this is putting too much strain on your life, you can ask the social worker to support you by arranging transport if the child is old enough, reducing the number of sessions, changing the time, asking another family member to help, or changing location.

If birth parents struggle to attend and commit to planned visits, you can make suggestions in writing to the parent to alter the time between sessions or give them alternative arrangements, such as phone/video calls or extending the time in between.

It is usual for children to develop new interests and spend more time with friends as they grow up. Consequently, they may spend less time with their birth parents, and they may want to stop seeing their birth parents altogether. Alternatively, some children may want to spend more time with their birth parents if it is safe to do so. Sometimes, they may even want to stay overnight or spend additional days with their birth parents. As the primary carer, it is your responsibility to make a safe and appropriate decision based on the child's best interest.

Contact orders are not written in stone; they can be changed, increased, or reduced if they are not in the child's best interests and cause them emotional, psychological or physical harm. It may be prudent to seek legal advice before making any changes to a contact order to ensure that you follow the proper steps and procedure.

5F: Supporting the Child Around Visits (Contact) With Birth Parents

When thinking about visits to birth parents or others (contact) with your connected child, it's important to hold the child's best interests at heart at all times. It might be the case that you really do not want to facilitate any of the visits and you are strongly opposed to them taking place.

If this is the case, try to separate out your own feelings towards the birth parents, and what the child's feelings and experiences might be. Ask yourself if the child is happy seeing their parents (or other family members), or if there seems to be clear behavioural indicators or other signs that the child is not happy and is suffering as a result.

One of the best ways we can support children in this situation is to make sure we are being very honest with them. It can be difficult to say what needs to be said. If there is a court order, and you are being forced to take the child on a visit against your will (and the child is not happy), it's okay to tell the child that the judge has made the decision, and this isn't something you want to do either. You don't need to collude with other people's poor decisions. Plan a nice treat for you both for afterwards.

We must also be very careful about the messages we are giving to the child if we (as the 'safe adult') take the child to see a person who is known to be unsafe or abusive to the child. When this happens, the person taking the child to a visit (which is experienced as abusive) is also perceived to be unsafe by the child. In our therapeutic fostering agencies at COECT, in these circumstances, the child is taken to the visit by a social worker, support worker or similar and the foster parent collects the child. In this way, we avoid giving mixed messages to the child and minimize the risk of causing a fracture in the parental therapeutic relationship.

Even when visiting family members is a positive experience, there may still be difficulties for the child before, during and after.

When the relationship is very positive this may reinforce a sense of loss. It's important that we acknowledge this with the child, and we give them time to readjust following visiting times. It's not always easy for the child to move between the conflicting loyalties they may feel towards birth parents and their kinship carers. Sometimes they will have difficult feelings and you might bear the brunt of this! At these times, it's important to tell the child that you understand what's happening. You might say, 'I know seeing your mum makes you feel wobbly, but that's normal, and I understand that.'

Discuss with the child what might be helpful for them in managing the aftermath or leading up to the visits. It's not a good idea to have these conversations when the visits are happening, so make sure you leave a good gap between a visit and discussions around practical arrangements. You can just acknowledge with the child that you know these visits are difficult and why they are difficult and then ask them for ideas or tell them your own ideas about how things can be made easier.

Last but not least, consider who is travelling to facilitate the visit and what is practical. It's not uncommon for arrangements to be made where the child is travelling long distances, but the adults are hardly expected to make any effort to travel for the visit. Sometimes this thinking is very entrenched, so it is vital to take a step back and ask the question, 'Why is the child having to travel all this distance each time, but the adults are staying near their home?' It is not child-centred planning, and needs to be challenged.

CHAPTER 6

A Changing Narrative: The Child's Story

Overview

Your connected child may have a complicated story. They will be relying on you to help them to make sense of their history. Sometimes you will have help from Social Services in this, and sometimes it can feel as if that isn't help at all! It may be that there is information being shared that you don't agree with.

Whatever the circumstances, it's important that we are honest, direct and straightforward with the child. The child will already be aware on some level of what has happened to them and will instinctively look for answers. It is our duty to ensure that our children understand what has happened, and that they are clear it was not their fault. In this way, we can help them to flourish and to overcome their early life trauma. This section explores different aspects of how we get the information we need and how it is shared.

6A: What Is the Child's Story?

Most kinship carers understand the child's past to some degree.

However, many kinship carers do not have information or only have it on a need-to-know basis. The primary goal of creating a child's story is to establish the facts; this will help the child understand and accept their history and avoid feeling ashamed or blaming themselves. The information should be placed to help the child understand their history and not feel overwhelmed.

It is vital to establish the facts about your kinship child's past. This can be done by requesting a chronological account of their history from their social worker. The report should include factual information, including the child's birth date, time and place of birth, birth weight and size, full name, and family members. It should also explain why the child was removed from their parents. Take time to read carefully through any information you receive. You can request this information from the post-order team if you don't have a social worker. Other ways to gather your kinship child's history include reviewing court papers, social worker reports and the child's red book. You could also speak to other relatives and the birth parents, depending on the circumstances.

It is essential to pay close attention to the reasons behind past decisions, which will enable you to provide a comprehensive understanding of your kinship child's history. This will help you determine what information to share and what the child may want to know now and in the future. When discussing these facts, keep the details honest, sensitive, simple and age appropriate. Importantly, it would be best to consider the child's safety and what information would be suitable and beneficial for them.

The primary goals of this process are to help the child understand and accept their history, avoid feeding into their sense of shame or self-blame, increase their self-esteem and self-worth, and give them a sense of a positive future. The narrative should be something the child can return to when they need to deal with their feelings and that will help them accept the past. It should also provide the words and structure for discussing happy memories.

6B: Ways of Communicating the Child's Story

[See also 11E: Who Am I Now?]

Sarah Naish writes: It isn't a great idea to sit a child down and give them all the bare facts of their life story without too much introduction! I always used 'the trickle of truth' to share the child's story in age-appropriate ways. There should never be a time when we are lying to the child. However, what a two-year-old can understand and reflect on is different from a 10- or 12-year-old.

I used lots of different ways to help my children understand their story. On one occasion, they wrote a letter to their birth parents telling them how they felt about them and sharing things that they remembered. These were not happy memories and the children processed quite a lot as they did this. I also learned things I didn't know as they wrote the stories. After they wrote the letters, we went into the garden, set fire to them, and watched the embers go up into the sky. The children found this very cathartic.

At other times, questions came up naturally. For example, when they came home from school and asked for a photo of them as a baby. In our situation, I did not have these photos, so I said, 'I don't have any photos of you as a baby. I wish I did have. The reason I don't have photos of you is because nobody took any photos and the ones that were there were thought to be a bit too sad.' I then went on to explain exactly what I meant by that.

In the early days, I used to encourage the children to draw pictures. They would draw pictures of the family and I helped them to draw the people in the right places, and in the right order, as it was often very muddled up. For example, their birth father was in prison, but one of my children drew him outside the house, as their fear was that he was watching us. We were able to draw a prison and put the birth father in there. The child was very happy about this.

Life story work is done in a way that is appropriate for the child's age and understanding. With my own adopted children, I would answer questions as they arose and I made sure my explanations were clear. I never vilified the birth parents, but I always gave the children the honest facts. I found that a useful phrase was to say to my children, 'Unfortunately there are some people who cannot parent children. This doesn't necessarily make them bad people, but they are just unable to do it.' I also used to say, 'I know this because they couldn't look after *you*, and you are the best children in the world, therefore we know they couldn't do it at all!'

By phrasing it in this way, we relieve the burden of guilt from the child. If we use terminology such as, 'Your parents couldn't look after YOU', the child hears YOU and may internalize that it was somehow their fault.

We also need to think about the words and phrases we use within the family to describe relationships. For example, your connected child may call you 'Mum', especially where there are other young children in the family. Using phrases like 'tummy mummy' to describe a birth mother can be a simple way to use honest explanation to a young child.

The important thing is not to shy away from difficulties, but keep the story factual, true and relevant. We can be sad with the child. We can grieve with them that we weren't there in the very early days if that was the case. We can share the wish that it would've been nice if we *had* been there. We can share our joint grief over missed opportunities, but we don't need to wallow in it. We need to make sure that our children feel like survivors and not victims and are able to see their survival through difficult circumstances as evidence of how strong and brave they are.

6C: Dealing With Input From Others (Child's Story)

[See also 5B: Blame and Judgement,
6E: Safety and Sharing Considerations]

It can sometimes be challenging to discuss the narrative of why children are not living with their parents. It can also be another challenge to discuss this with extended family, even more so when the true story conflicts with that of the birth parents.

Emma is a kinship carer with a Child Arrangement Order for her grandson, James, which was completed under a private arrangement. Emma was concerned that James might be placed in foster care if social workers became involved. Her daughter Lucy was struggling with drug addiction and was unable to care for James properly. Emma and Lucy agreed to ensure James's safety and well-being by Emma taking James home to live with her. It was several months before Emma would see Lucy again, and it was not to see James but to ask for money. This went on for many years. Emma's extended family knew that James lived with her, and they had a rough idea of why, but they never thoroughly discussed it. Emma never entirely told friends the whole story. She did not mind what others thought. She aimed to explain the truth to James when he was old enough to understand. As James got older, she told him the whole truth, which he accepted.

Lucy's narrative of events differed significantly from the truth. She informed her relatives and friends that she had asked Emma to care for James during a weekend break. However, when she returned, Emma refused to return James, claiming that she had intended to keep him as she had always wanted another child.

Some kinship carers carry the shame of their adult children or relatives who were responsible for causing harm or neglect to their kinship child. Or they are so angry with the birth parent's actions and are not concerned about holding back on the whole truth or perhaps, like Emma, believe that one day the truth will be told.

It is true that some people who are not part of the family, or close family friends, will suddenly feel they have a right to know all the gory details! They don't. It's fine to say, 'I'm sorry, that is private family information that we do not share.' Always be clear that this story really belongs to the child and their birth parents. We need to be respectful of that, while also ensuring that the child is clear about events that have happened.

Honesty is the best policy!

The truth will always be the best outcome. You don't necessarily have to explain the details to others; they don't need to know everything. Most importantly, you must be mindful of the harm it may cause your kinship child. Dealing with a birth parent who lies or changes the story can be very challenging. You must realize you cannot change their behaviour but can control how you respond. Establish your boundaries with them, communicate openly with the birth parent if you can, and explain to them how their behaviour will negatively affect their child and others around them.

6D: Life Story Books

When children have had complicated early starts in life, they rely on us to help them to make sense about what's happened to them.

The most important aspects of giving a child their life story is that of honesty. Sometimes a social worker might be involved in producing a 'life story book'.

I've often had kinship carers speak to me about the contents of the life story book saying that they feel that what is in the book doesn't necessarily reflect what has happened to the child. If it doesn't resonate with you, then it won't resonate with the child!

We need to remember that even if our connected children do not remember what happened to them on a cognitive level, their body will hold those trauma memories. If we give them a watered-down version of the truth, then they will know. If it does not feel right to them, then they may lose trust in their relationship with you.

If your child has a life story book, make sure that you are happy about what it says and that the contents are true. You also need to make sure that the book is kept in a place where the child has age-appropriate access. We never advise that life story books are kept in the child's bedroom because we never know what this might trigger.

As a kinship carer, you are uniquely placed, in that you may hold a lot of the child's history. For example, there will still be members of the family around who are related to the child so the extensive life story can be consistent. You just have to make sure that you are clear about why the child is living with you and what happened to make that the case.

6E: Safety and Sharing Considerations

[See also 6C: Dealing with Input From Others (Child's Story)]

As a kinship carer, although it is important to clearly understand the reasons and details behind your child's story, including their experiences and the impact this has had on their lives, it is also essential to exercise discretion and consider privacy and safety when discussing or sharing any information with those who come into contact with you and the child. Sharing information should be limited to only those who require it to support you or the child.

Sometimes, sharing certain information with close family members or support networks who regularly interact with your kinship child, such as babysitters, youth workers, teachers or medical professionals, might be necessary. However, *only share information on a need-to-know basis and always respect the child or young person's confidentiality*. Please remember that some young people may not want their information disclosed to professionals or others, so it is best to discuss this with them first.

As a connected foster carer, you have to follow the local authority rules, such as you do not have permission to discuss your kinship child's information without consent from the local authority or the birth parents. You may not be permitted to share information or photographs on any social media platform such as Facebook, Instagram or other websites.

Depending on your circumstances, you have the right to withhold your personal information, such as your address, from anyone connected to your kinship child, such as birth parents or their extended family. Likewise, you do not have the right to share their information either.

As a kinship carer, you do not have the same rules as a connected foster carer in relation to information sharing. You have parental responsibility along with the birth parents. However, it's always critical to be mindful of what information you share. It's worth remembering that birth parents still have parental responsibility, which means you cannot stop them from sharing information about their children unless they are legally prevented from doing so by the courts.

Points to consider

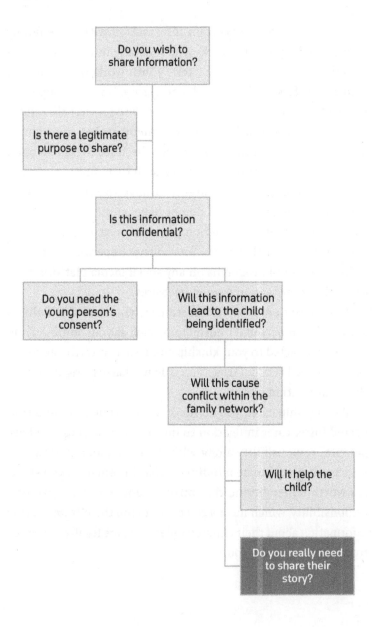

CHAPTER 7

Difficult Feelings – Feeling Better

Overview

As kinship carers, we are exposed to a myriad of conflicting emotions and difficulties. Kinship carers have often told us that they have felt abandoned and lost. The loss of their planned future and the breakdown of relationships with birth parents contribute significantly to these difficulties.

For some, this can be the first time that they have had direct dealings with Social Services. It can feel extremely frustrating to cooperate with Social Services when their views conflict with ours. This is particularly hard when we are hearing information about our own birth children, perhaps the adult parents of our now connected child.

All of this breeds resentment and can lead to withdrawal and compassion fatigue. When we have compassion fatigue we're not in a very good state to carry on giving the much-needed nurture and empathy to our children.

This chapter looks at how we can recognize these difficult feelings and what we can do about them.

7A: Guilt

[See also 7G: Essential Maintenance (Self-Care)]

Guilt is a difficult, complex and challenging topic for many of us, and it is one of the many uncomfortable emotions that kinship carers often struggle with. Occasionally, we can all face a personal battle and constantly question our actions and decisions. We may have thoughts such as, 'Should I have intervened sooner?' or, 'Could I have helped more?' or, 'How did I miss the signs?'

Many kinship carers share that they experience parental guilt when it comes to their children causing harm or neglect, and they find it challenging to stop these feelings. Some carers ask the question, 'Am I to blame for my grandchild being with me?' Furthermore, we may feel guilty for being unable to take on another sibling or feeling as if we have reached our limit. It is also understandable to experience guilt for knowing that the birth parent is heartbroken, and that this situation may not be entirely their fault.

Guilt is a common emotion, but it is important to remember that it doesn't necessarily mean you've done something wrong. Like all feelings, guilt affects how we think, feel, speak and act. But the truth is, guilt is a completely normal emotion, like all other feelings. It is what we do with these feelings that matters most.

Here's what you can do:

- Identify your triggers to help you understand the thoughts that make you feel guilty and help you handle them in a better way.
- If you notice unhelpful thoughts that make you feel guilty, consciously reframe them more positively.
- Do not isolate yourself; instead, build a support system of trusted family and friends you can rely on.
- Practise self-care (see 7G: Essential Maintenance (Self-

Care)) and being compassionate and kind to yourself. Taking occasional breaks can help you recharge your batteries.

- Find a kinship support group, as sharing your experience with others who have walked in your shoes will lighten the load.
- Seek professional help. If you find that you're unable to cope and frequently experience feelings of guilt, despair, depression or anxiety, seek out therapy to help manage your mindset and find a better balance in your life.

7B: Grief and Loss

It's perfectly normal to feel a mix of emotions when you're suddenly thrust into the role of a kinship carer. On one hand, you have the opportunity to provide a stable and loving home for a growing child, which can be incredibly fulfilling. On the other hand, you may feel a sense of grief or loss.

Regardless of the order, every kinship carer will feel some grief or loss at some point. It could be the loss of their planned future life, the loss of a relationship with a birth parent, or the loss of their own identity as they become a parent instead of a grandparent, uncle/aunt, family friend. It's never easy to talk about loss; kinship carers often feel a deep sense of loss in many different ways.

Enza Smith writes: This is probably one of the most challenging sections in this book for me. We planned to have our children in our younger adult life; we took them on fantastic child-focused holidays; we planned our careers, worked hard and saved money for our future. We planned that once our children had grown up, moved out and got on with their lives, we would be young enough to plan life, hobbies and holidays around us. What we did not factor in was becoming kinship carers. We had to use all our hard-earned savings to raise our grandchildren, put aside our plans, leave our jobs because of my health and the difficulties of kinship care, and then lose my friends, and sadly lose my husband, and this was all before we got to retirement. Unfortunately, I understand your journey and have walked in your shoes.

So, how did I deal with it? I first accepted my new life and then learned to embrace it. I made new dreams with my grandchildren. Second, I worked through the emotions I experienced, which allowed me to manage them better and stay emotionally balanced. I still have my down days, and I am by no means perfect. However, I can get through the bad days with God's grace.

Tips to help you through your sense of grief or loss

- Make time to look after yourself, including your emotional and physical health.
- Look at ways to improve your self-care.
- Take time to rest.
- Focus on the positives.
- Accept the change.
- Make time to be with the friends who make you smile.
- See your GP or get support from a trusted counsellor.
- Make new achievable plans and memories.

Remember, you are not alone; join a support group and meet others like you and those who have walked your path. We have made some suggestions for this in 1I: Where Can I Go for Help?

7C: Differences of Opinion

[See also 2H: What if I'm Not Happy?]

It's not uncommon for people to have varying opinions. However, when issues arise, it is essential to listen to other people's opinions; they may bring different experiences and perspectives, we may be able to see things in a new light and adjust our views, or it may give us more reason to believe we are right and defend our opinions. It's not uncommon for social workers, carers and birth parents to disagree on specific issues, and conflicting beliefs can sometimes create tension, especially when we feel unheard or think the other person's views could be harmful or wrong. In situations like this, conflicts may arise and need to be resolved quickly.

Here are some ideas that might help to balance this conflict:

- When dealing with conflicting opinions, separating the issue from the person(s) involved is essential. This will help you deal with the evidence and facts.
- Manage your emotions and control your reactions.
- Listen to other people's opinions and write down key points for discussion.
- Take a few deep breaths, pause before responding and keep your tone calm.
- On occasion, you may need to process the information and discuss it on a different day.
- Avoid blaming or criticizing others.
- Clearly express your thoughts and feelings.
- Use simple language and short sentences to make your message clear and easy to understand.
- Above all, outcomes must always be based on the best interests of the child.

What happens if your opinion is not taken seriously by the social worker?

If your social worker isn't listening, ask for a separate meeting. You can take an advocate such as a friend to the meeting. Although they may not be allowed to comment, it may help to have someone with you. If you still think your option is not heard and feel it needs acting on, put it in writing and email both the social worker and their manager. We have written more about this in 2H: What if I'm Not Happy?

What happens if your opinion is not taken seriously by birth parents?

If you feel birth parents have a difference of opinion and this is not in the child's best interests, first, be honest with them and try to discuss the issue. If the situation is not acceptable, set clear boundaries and expectations. If it is safe to do so, arrange a meeting, or a phone call, and if it's not safe, send an email. If it is a serious situation and cannot be resolved, you may need help from outside agencies such as mediation services, or Social Services if they are still involved, or ask a third party to help.

7D: Anger

[See also 7G: Essential Maintenance (Self-Care)]

What an emotive word anger is… It can trigger the fight response in us and then trigger other responses, such as fear, anxiety or excitement. Our bodies can also experience stress hormones, affecting our muscles, heart rate and blood pressure, or trigger a flight response where we try to run away.

Kelly's daughter had severe postnatal depression after her first baby and she unsuccessfully self-medicated; her GP admitted her to a psychiatric hospital for treatment. Children's services got involved and placed the baby in a foster-to-adopt placement. Kelly fought hard to become a kinship carer; she passed her assessment, medical and references. It was a difficult struggle as everyone seemed against her. Kelly was angry with her daughter for not reaching out to her, angry at the GP for not informing her, angry with the social worker who seemed determined to place her grandchild up for adoption, angry towards the courts for dragging the case out, and angry with herself for not stepping in earlier.

The case took a year and a half to conclude, and Kelly's health deteriorated during this time. The effects of this situation left Kelly in a state of desperation. She went to see her GP, who provided her with counselling. Kelly put some self-care strategies in place. She also joined a support group and spoke to other carers with similar experiences. Kelly worked out that forgiveness was her powerful tool. She found that she allowed anger and different negative feelings to crowd out all her positive emotions and found herself swallowed up by the sense of bitterness and injustice. Forgiving people who angered her helped her learn from the situation and strengthened her relationship with her daughter.

The final court date came, and Kelly took her grandchild home with an SGO. Six years after this, Kelly's daughter has recovered, got married, had another child, and built up her relationship with her child. Kelly now shares the care of her grandchild.

Health problems that you may experience if continuous feelings of anger are not dealt with

- Headache
- Digestion problems, such as abdominal pain
- Insomnia
- Increased anxiety
- Depression
- High blood pressure
- Skin problems, such as eczema
- Heart attack
- Stroke.

Tips and ideas to help you cope

- See your GP if you are feeling the physical effects of anger.
- Join support groups with other kinship carers.
- Verbalize your feelings; talk to a counsellor, partner or trusted friend.
- Write down your feelings if you think you cannot talk about them.
- Do gentle or aerobic exercises, such as walking, dancing, running and gardening.
- Visit a church or museum.
- Take time out, lie down and listen to some pleasant, relaxing music.

7E: Resentment

Resentment is a familiar feeling that we can experience at any stage in our lives. It's natural to feel resentful when expectations, hopes and dreams are unmet. Kinship carers often experience this emotion due to the difficult circumstances they encounter, such as feeling they are being taken advantage of or feeling unrecognized or unappreciated.

Resentment may arise from:

- the belief that someone has been wronged, such as a kinship child mistreated by their birth parents
- not receiving the support and finances you are entitled to
- feeling that others around you don't 'get it'
- the birth parents putting you in this situation intentionally or not
- the impact on other children in the family, having to go without to make ends meet
- suddenly having a lot more strain on your finances.

Resentment can have a significant impact on the entire family and can even put a strain on a couple's relationship. Therefore, it is crucial to recognize and understand that these emotions need to be addressed so you can effectively move towards a healthier emotional state. Doing so can foster stronger relationships within the family and improve overall well-being.

Here are a few steps that may help you let go of resentment:

- **Don't retaliate or avoid things:** When we feel resentment, it's understandable to want to restore justice or try to ignore it. But both of these actions can ultimately do more harm than good. Instead, try to focus on positive, constructive changes within yourself. This can help you overcome resentment and create a more fulfilling and satisfying life.
- **Check your entitlement:** If you find yourself feeling resentful after a situation, it's essential to take a moment to reflect on your expectations. Ask yourself if you might have had unrealistic or unfair expectations. Were you expecting special treatment, or did you feel someone owed you something? By identifying any mismatches between your expectations and what was likely to happen, you can take steps to reduce your resentment and move forward.
- **Accept what happened:** The past is beyond your control, but you can control your present reaction. Embrace acceptance as a tool to help you achieve this.
- **Forgive what you can:** Don't take it personally; most mistakes in life are unintentional. People usually try their best, even if they end up hurting you. So, it's better to forgive and move on.
- **Find something to be grateful for:** This might involve looking for a silver lining in a difficult situation or helping you find a different aspect of the problem. Focusing on the positives enables you to cope better with stressful

situations, reducing stress's harmful health effects on your body.

Resentment vs forgiveness

Forgiveness is close to the opposite of resentment. When you forgive somebody, you accept the situation as it is, letting go of your attachment to how unfair it felt. Forgiveness and resentment can't co-exist – you're experiencing one or the other.

7F: Compassion Fatigue

Sarah Naish writes: You might have heard the expression 'compassion fatigue'. It's a very good explanation in itself! It literally means tired of caring. It's very normal for people who are caring for children who have additional needs to suffer from compassion fatigue.

How do you know if you have it? Well, the first signs are that you withdraw from the child. You start to find excuses about why you don't want to be with them. Maybe you are spending longer at work, maybe you are finding lots of things for the child to do in their bedroom? Don't get me wrong, we all need these little breaks, otherwise how would we carry on?

The difference with compassion fatigue is that it gets worse and worse. Research was conducted by Bristol University and our training company (part of the Centre of Excellence in Child Trauma) in 2016 about compassion fatigue (Ottaway & Selwyn, 2016). The research found that foster parents suffered high rates of compassion fatigue.

Anecdotally, my experience is that the rates appear higher in kinship care because the support, generally, is less.

If you find that you are:

- struggling to access empathy for your child

- feeling 'burnt out'
- feeling as if you don't want to carry on
- wanting to avoid your child

...it's likely that you have compassion fatigue.

The first thing to understand is that this is *normal*. Compassion fatigue is a real physiological condition. The good news is that there are lots of things that will help you to overcome this. I'll be talking about this in 7G: Essential Maintenance (Self-Care).

It's important to make sure you can talk to other people who understand how you are feeling and will listen to you without blame or judgement – 'empathic listening' in other words.

We also need to look after ourselves, so our next section is on this. By using essential maintenance, you can keep yourself out of compassion fatigue, or at least minimize the effects.

7G: Essential Maintenance (Self-Care)

Sarah Naish writes: I often hear people talking about self-care and I've spoken about that myself in the past. Self-care sounds really fluffy and something that's an optional extra. These days, I prefer to think about 'essential maintenance'. If you don't have oil in the car, the car will grind to a halt. By simply doing a little bit of work to preserve yourself, you can keep going. The simple act of adding oil to the car, even though it takes five minutes, means that the engine won't explode – and it's the same for us.

It isn't self-indulgent or wasteful to make sure we look after ourselves. After all, who is going to look after the children if we can no longer continue?

First of all, we have to have perspective on our situation. The best breakthrough moments I had when I suddenly got inspiration were always times when I was away from the children. It's very difficult to plan a war if you're always fighting in the trenches. I'm not saying that living with our children and caring for them should be a war, but sometimes it does feel like that!

We need that longer view. If you stand too close to a picture, all you can see are the little dots; it's only when you step away that you see the bigger picture. It's the same for our lived-in situation. We need perspective.

This is easier said than done though. How do we get a break? This could be something as simple as an hour here and there when the children are at school. A coffee with a friend or supportive other, or it might even extend to going away for the night, leaving the children with somebody who can look after them in your own home.

The break is much more important than making sure that everything goes exactly as you would want it to go. Yes okay, things may be done differently when you're not there, but if you're there all the time you will gradually grind to a complete halt.

Getting a break takes planning. You need to look ahead and plan when you're going to take this time for yourself. Just knowing it is safely there in the diary can often keep us going.

Other strategies that therapeutic parents have found incredibly helpful are using mindfulness techniques to reduce stress. In *The A–Z of Survival Strategies* (Naish, 2022) I explain all about this and all the strategies I used to keep going and to reduce stress.

In 7F: Compassion Fatigue, I mentioned empathic listening. Everybody needs to have somebody who will listen to them without judgement and blame. When we are in compassion fatigue, or in danger of being in compassion fatigue, a good old chat over a coffee and off-loading all the ways of the world really does change the brain chemistry and relieve stress. It's not a waste of time and it isn't self-indulgent. Think of these little oases of 'you time' as oil in your car.

The National Association of Therapeutic Parents provides an empathic listening service to members if you are unable to find a like-minded other. Through them, you can also contact

The Haven Parenting and Wellbeing Centre. They are excellent at providing meaningful, targeted support for all therapeutic parents and understand the stresses you are dealing with: www. naotp.com .

CHAPTER 8

Working With Others

Overview

When you start caring for a connected child, whatever the situation, there will suddenly be a lot of expectations and new responsibilities. In this chapter, we explain clearly what the expectations will be and how they differ depending on:

- the differing legal statuses
- the social work team you are working with
- the local authority where you live
- your relationship to the birth parents.

It might be that you are wondering how you're going to learn all the information that you suddenly need, or in fact you might be feeling the opposite. Perhaps you are struggling to understand why on earth you would need training or more information to care for a family member! This is particularly relevant to people who have been fostering a child as a professional foster carer for some time, and have then chosen to go the SGO route.

The legislation around kinship fostering is clear. We have to keep records and we have to share those records to make sure that the state is doing its job and that the children are safe. However resentful we may be, there's not really a way round it.

It is important to know what you need to do and why, but also to explore how you can get the support and advocacy you need when you do not agree with the decisions being made. In this chapter, we help you understand who may be involved and how we all work together.

8A: Responsibilities and Expectations

(See also 2B: What Documents Should I Have?, 8C: Record Keeping)

As a kinship carer, regardless of the legal order, you have a significant responsibility and expectation to provide a loving, safe and nurturing home for the children in your care. You also play a critical role in ensuring that their physical and mental well-being needs are met.

You may need to register your child with the following to ensure that their health and social well-being needs are met:

- GP practice – including immunizations
- Dentist
- Opticians
- Health visitor
- Necessary hospital appointments
- Therapeutic appointments.

Depending on the age of your kinship children, you need to ensure they attend suitable education and activities:

- Nursery
- School
- College
- Extracurricular clubs.

You will also need to ensure that your kinship children are available and have the opportunity to spend quality time with their birth parents and perhaps other family members, according to your legal agreement.

As a kinship carer, you hold an essential position in your child's life. You are their advocate, their voice and their protector. You can shape their future and help them become the best version of themselves. Your guidance, support and encouragement are vital to their growth and success. You will make a significant difference by actively participating in your child's life.

Most importantly, you can enjoy creating happy memories and participating in normal family activities.

However, this is where the similarities end between kinship carers and connected foster carers. For connected carers, you are expected to:

- keep a log/diary of events which you submit to the local authority
- attend looked-after child (LAC) meetings
- attend Personal Education Planning (PEP) meetings
- attend meetings with the child social worker
- attend meetings with your supporting social worker
- attend training to develop your skills
- potentially be responsible for supervising contact/family time with birth parents, according to agreed arrangements
- attend the fostering panels
- notify the local authority of significant changes and events, such as moving home, marriage or separation, or emergency hospital admission
- work closely with your child's social worker if your child is attending a new educational setting, as the local authority has parental responsibility and must complete all necessary forms.

To learn more about your responsibilities and expectations as a foster carer, please read the detailed guidelines of *The National Minimum Standards*, which can be found on the UK Government website, www.gov.uk.

Essentially, by providing a nurturing environment and showing love, care and support, you have the power to positively impact the lives of the children in your care. With your guidance and encouragement, you can help them build the bright, happy future they truly deserve!

8B: Training

It might seem like a bit of a strange idea that you need 'training' to look after your connected child. If you're lucky, your local authority will include you in the training with the adopters and foster parents for that local authority.

Unfortunately, some kinship carers are told that they 'don't need training', because the child is related to them and therefore they should somehow instinctively know what to do. This is not the case. Trauma is trauma, and trauma means that there are often challenging and perplexing behaviours. You may well find that you have a lot in common with people who are fostering or have adopted, although of course the legal situation is different.

It's definitely worthwhile asking your local authority if you can be included in any training for adopters and foster parents, especially relating to managing conflict, trauma and resulting behaviours.

If you cannot access the information and training easily, then visit the Centre of Excellence in Child Trauma and have a look at our website, www.coect.co.uk. You will see we have lots of online training, qualifications and face-to-face workshops that are run in different places. We even have a Level 1 qualification designed specifically for kinship carers. You can also contact the National

Association of Therapeutic Parents (www.naotp.com) and see if they are delivering training soon to your local authority. We are often able to invite kinship carers along.

Kinship Carers UK also offer free webinars and support groups which include training: www.kinshipcarersuk.com.

8C: Record Keeping

[See also 1D: Essential Things First, 8A: Responsibilities and Expectations]

Enza Smith writes: After our house move, we had lots of paper-work in boxes, which we put in the loft until we had time to go through them. My husband needed his birth certificate for his DBS, which happened to be in one of the boxes. So, he decided to get a new one rather than spend hours sorting through boxes. It was only then he found out that he was adopted. Unfortunately, his parents had passed away, and we thought that was the end. He then contacted our local authority to see if they had a record of the start of his life. Fortunately, there was a clear record; his foster carers and adoptive parents had made notes, and he was able to piece his early life together and meet siblings he never knew he had.

As a 'connected foster carer', you must keep a log (diary) of the day's events. It is a good idea for all carers to keep a diary, regardless of legal order, as it may serve you well in the future. Some carers use the log to record part of the children's life story book of beautiful memories and events they have experienced together. Don't forget to take lots of memorable photographs!

The log/diary can be used to:

- record information about a child's life

- measure and reflect on any significant changes in the child
- aid decision-making, assessments, reports and reviews
- protect the carer and family from false allegations
- record parental family time
- record significant events, milestones and achievements.

The main aim of daily logs is to keep detailed facts on record and ensure that you remember what is happening during your busy life. For example:

- **Family time/visits/contact:** Dates and times with birth family when they occur or any other form of contact, including how your child was before and afterwards.
- **Social work appointments:** Dates and times of visits with social workers, meetings, visits and any other reviews. You should also note what was discussed, who said what and what was agreed, as minutes are not always completed on time and may not include things that you believe are important.
- **Health appointments:** Any illnesses, including symptoms and medication, visits with the doctor, dates of any vaccinations or immunizations, and routine check-ups with dentists and other healthcare professionals.
- **Notable incidents:** Anything that occurs during the day that you consider an incident. This might be to do with behaviour if your kin child is acting strangely, refusing to eat or showing other unusual behaviours.
- **Educational issues:** Any struggles with school, as well as meetings with teachers and teacher comments.
- **Disclosures:** Any information the child discloses that you have not heard, no matter how severe or minor.
- **General well-being:** A general record of health, activities and hobbies.

8D: Meetings

We completely understand that being a kinship carer can be quite demanding and you have to manage a lot of responsibilities simultaneously. From taking care of your kinship child to maintaining a work and family life, as well as attending numerous routine appointments and meetings, it can all feel overwhelming, especially if you're a connected foster carer. It may seem as if you have a full-time job managing meetings and appointments. We sympathize with how challenging it can be to balance everything and how tiring it can be to juggle these responsibilities constantly. Please remember that the duration between each meeting varies for each local authority and depends on your personal circumstances.

Type of meeting	Explanation
Children's social work visit	Social workers for children ensure their well-being and safety. They meet carers every six weeks or once every three months for long-term stays.
Family group conference	A family-led meeting in which the family and friends network to make a plan for a child. An independent coordinator supports the process.
Independent Reviewing Officer (IRO) meeting/review	IROs are responsible for monitoring the progress of the care plan, ensuring there is no drift or delay in achieving permanence. These reviews occur at different intervals depending on how long the child has been in care, but are held at least every six months.
Looked-after child review	A scheduled meeting that brings together professionals closely involved with you and your child. It is an opportunity to review your child's care plan, discuss progress and make plans.

Supervision meeting for the carer	Supervision should be reflective, enabling foster carers to share their thoughts and views and receive support. Meetings with carers take place every six weeks or once every three months for long-term stays.
Medical for children	The designated doctor or nurse leads medical assessments every six months for children under five and annually for children aged 5–18. They evaluate physical, dental and visual health, developmental growth, diagnosis/medical conditions, and sexual health for those over 13.
Medical for carer	Connected foster carers must undergo a medical examination to be approved, and have regular medical check-ups every three years throughout their careers.
Fostering panel meeting	Thoroughly evaluates potential foster carers to determine their suitability to perform this role. Connected foster carers are reviewed at least once a year, with the first annual review taking place within 12 months of their approval or six months of a child being placed, whichever occurs sooner.
Personal Education Plan meeting	Held every term for children in care. It focuses on the child's education and any experiences that may impact it.

8E: But What About Me?

Right from the beginning of our journey of becoming kinship carers, we are subjected to much scrutiny. We must answer questions about ourselves and justify our past and present actions. Then, we are told we must fill out all sorts of paperwork. We are then pushed into attending meetings for this, that and the other, and our voices and opinions are documented. Unsurprisingly, we feel exhausted as we try to comply with every demand and abide by many unseen and unknown rules that change as quickly as they are explained.

Debbie works full time and cares for two children. She was seemingly supported by two young social workers, both of whom had just finished university and were younger than the birth parents; one had an unrealistic, idealistic view of the world and the other had abysmal note-taking skills and an awful attitude. Debbie felt unsupported by both social workers, especially when she was told that she had to supervise family time with both birth parents, who were heavily into substance misuse, and this was supposed to be done after she had finished work. Debbie asked if family time could be moved to a weekend when everyone was not so rushed and tired. She was then subjected to untold abuse and reported. She was threatened with having her grandchildren removed and then subjected to an early fostering panel as she was told she was not putting the children first.

Not knowing what to do, Debbie contacted Kinship Carers UK, the National Union of Professional Foster Carers and the Foster Care Workers Union. They told her what her rights were and offered support. Through them, she learned more about being a foster carer than the social workers had led her to believe. She was directed to the National Fostering Standards, where she discovered she had been misled and misinformed. Debbie was also accompanied to the panel meeting with an advocate, where she was told her care of the children was exemplary, and she was passed for another year.

Enza Smith writes: I want to share what I have learned about working with others:

- Remember that it's okay to disagree and express your opinions, and it is a good idea to put them in writing.
- Keep clear records of all meetings and ensure that all meeting minutes are correct and that you have the final copy.

- Take an advocate with you to meetings; this can be a friend or a professional. It makes a big difference.
- It's okay to request new social workers (I did this and I now work with two wonderful and supportive social workers).
- Remember that if you are unsure of what you are being told, contact Kinship Carers UK or organizations such as Foster Wiki, The Fostering Network or your Fostering Union.
- Download the National Minimum Standards for fostering services.
- Build a support team around you of professionals and friends, and join support groups; you can learn so much from other carers.

CHAPTER 9

It's Not About the Money, but...

Overview

When there is such a big change in circumstances, finances change too! Very often we hear that kinship carers don't like to talk about money and feel that they must bear all the financial burden. This is a natural feeling when the child is related to you, and you feel that love and responsibility. However, we *do* need to be a bit assertive here. Remember that if you were not looking after this child they may well be in the care system. This would cost the local authority a great deal of money. Adoption, fostering and children's homes are not cheap. While that's not the driving factor, you will definitely have suffered significant financial losses and changes and also be having to make alterations to your long-term plans. There is no reason why you should not be assertive, think about how your standard of living has changed and ask for help with that.

Sometimes we don't think about the implications of financial changes in the future, but we must look forward and consider the impact on pensions, benefits and entitlements, and anything the child might be entitled to as well. If you are having to pay for childcare, this cost can be very significant. In this chapter, we look at what help you can get and how you go about accessing it.

9A: Life Has Changed!

When we deliver training, many kinship carers speak to us and say that they wished they had known before what they know now. The truth of the matter is (as you probably already know), your life changes beyond all recognition.

In Chapter 9, we explain how your finances change. However, finances aside, *life* is not going to be the same again.

It's really important that you take the bull by the horns and look long and hard at the impact on your finances, your standard of living and the way you run your life. In meeting these challenges head on, and being clear about what your needs are, you can really help to smooth the path in the future.

Many kinship carers have said they 'don't like to rock the boat', or that they don't like to ask for things in case there is a threat to remove the child. This is very unlikely to happen, as Social Services invariably would like the child to stay with you.

It is not unreasonable to point out that you now have to work part time and you have a lot less money. It's perfectly fine to state that you have had to dig into your pension. What's going to happen in the future when you've used a lot more of your pension and the children are teenagers? Children don't become cheaper.

As soon as you are thinking about having your connected child coming to live with you full time, you need to take a good long look at your current standard of living. Think about what might change and how you can mitigate those changes. You may need to think about things like:

- holidays
- vehicles
- who is at home
- who works, and what their hours are
- who is available for the school run
- how the practical needs of the children will be funded.

All of these issues will impact on your standard of living. This may well be a price you are happy to pay, but it is completely okay to let those assessing you know that this impact has happened. By being open and transparent about the costs that are involved and the impact on your lifestyle, it can help you get a fair assessment of your financial needs for the future.

In Chapter 10: Making a Plan, we spell out a lot of the separate items which you need to think about and cost out. Whatever your legal situation, and whatever the future looks like, this is a very useful prompt sheet to look at and help you think about what your needs are now and how they might change.

9B: Entitlements

When considering financial support now and in the future, it is essential to investigate what you and your child will be entitled to, the kind of support, and how you will manage. You must take the initiative and reach out to your local authority and ask for their kinship handbook and funding policy so you can make informed decisions. Remember that every local authority offers varying support and finances, which can appear discriminative for various orders, so it's imperative to understand what you can expect from the start.

The level of financial support you receive depends on various factors, such as the local authority you live in, how much they value kinship care and if the local authority has adequate finances. If you are a connected foster carer, you must receive the national minimum fostering allowance. Some local authorities pay above the national minimum fostering allowance, which may be equal to that of stranger foster carers. Once you move to an SGO, you may get the same allowance for two years before being means-tested unless you negotiate a better support plan.

Similar discrimination also applies to SGO and CAO allowances. Receiving support payments for your child is determined by several factors, including whether your child is a previously looked-after child, the strength of your support plan, your negotiation skills, and your local authority's policies.

What about the children?

- **Adoption and Specialist Guardian Support Fund:** This offers therapeutic support for previously looked-after children only. The SGO post-order team can access this fund.
- **Pupil Premium Plus:** This is a fund used by schools in England to help improve educational outcomes for children currently or previously looked after by the local authority.
- **Virtual Schools:** These support children aged 2–18 who were previously or are currently in the care system to improve their education outcomes. They may offer advice and support to SGO and CAO carers and attend meetings with you to speak to the school about your concerns. Contact details for Virtual Schools can be found on your local authority's website.

Benefits

Due to the continual changes in benefits, going to the primary source is always helpful. Please take a look at the following:

- Benefits for Families: www.gov.uk/browse/benefits/families
- Childcare: www.gov.uk/get-childcare
- Families on low income: www.gov.uk/browse/benefits/low-income.

Independent advice

You can use an independent, free, anonymous benefits calculator to check your entitlement: www.gov.uk/benefits-calculators.

This will give you an estimate of:

- the benefits you might be entitled to
- how much your benefit payments could be
- how your benefits will be affected if you start work or increase your hours
- how your benefits will be affected if your circumstances change; for example, if you have a child move in with you.

Independent sources

For free, up-to-date, independent financial advice about benefits and grants available, visit www.turn2us.org.uk or www.citizens-advice.org.uk.

9C: Who Pays?

If the local authority makes the arrangements for a relative's or friend's child to live in your care, the local authority is responsible for supporting that placement. Also, birth parents remain financially responsible for their children and, if agreed, pay child maintenance. If you can speak with the parents, try to reach an agreement. If this is not possible, you can apply to the Child Maintenance Service at www.gov.uk/child-maintenance-service.

Private law orders can include allowances that are reviewed annually and means-tested based on the local authority's policy. If your circumstances change, your allowance may also vary accordingly unless it is written in your SGO or CAO support plan. It is essential to check your local authority's policy, as local authorities may only award these allowances for a limited period.

Section 17 of the Children Act 1989 states that financial

assistance can be provided to families if the health and safety of the child are severely affected without support. The assessment explores all potential sources of financial aid. Any payment agreement will consider any funding sources or benefit entitlements you or the child may have. If the parents are unwilling to contribute or transfer benefits, the local authority may cover the difference until the issue is resolved.

Quick guide

Type of care order	Who pays	Information about the payment
Connected foster carers	Local authority (LA)	Fostering allowances are paid regardless of income, and increase with the child's age. Looked-after children always come within the definition of Children in Need, if they are accommodated under Section 20 of the Children Act 1989.
Child arrangement order (CAO)	Local authority	The LA may assess you under Section 17 of the Children Act 1989 if they have placed the child with you. However, financial support may be discretionary, means-tested and not mandatory.
	Birth parents	Apply directly or via child maintenance support.
Private arrangement	Local authority	The LA may assess your eligibility for financial assistance under Section 17 of the Children Act. Note that assistance is subject to means-testing, discretionary and not mandatory.
	Birth parents	Apply directly or via child maintenance support.

cont.

Type of care order	Who pays	Information about the payment
Special Guardianship Order	Local authority	Special Guardianship Allowance may be subject to a means test. This covers one-time expenses and regular ongoing assistance. However, not every carer will be approved for this allowance. The allowance amount is determined based on the local authority's policy and child benefits, including universal credit. It may be reviewed on an annual basis and reduced or terminated. Sometimes, it is only granted for a specific length of time unless otherwise stated in your support plan.
	Birth parents	Apply directly or via child maintenance support.

9D: Forward Planning: Unexpected Financial Changes

[See also 9B: Entitlements]

Sarah Naish writes: Just as when we parented first time around we had to budget and plan for the future, the same can be said for our changing circumstances now.

It's important that we look at all the entitlements we have now, but then also look at what future entitlements there might be. For example, it may be that your child will be entitled to disability living allowance or some other help. It could be that the birth parents are contributing to the maintenance costs of the child. We have to think about whether that can always be relied on and what we might do if that changes. For example, I didn't know that Disability Living Allowance ended when my child turned 16, as if somehow their disability had magically disappeared! We have to keep on top of these things and make sure we are making the right applications in a timely way. The Citizens Advice Bureau can help you with this.

If you have been granted a Special Guardianship Order it is likely that you will be awarded financial help, but this may well be for a short time only. It is essential that you check the order and plan for the future. For example, if you are only receiving funding from the local authority for the next two years, how old will the child be in two years and what does this mean for your working life?

In kinship fostering, you are likely to be receiving an equivalent fostering allowance, but again, keep on top of any proposed changes to this from the local authority.

It's also interesting to note that *costs* might be significantly higher when looking after children from trauma. I noticed that my children went through clothes and shoes at a much quicker rate than other children. There were higher levels of damage and generally a disregard for their own possessions. It's very common for children who have suffered trauma to have very little regard for their own things. Frequently, clothing or equipment is lost, which may need to be replaced. At the same time, we may feel that we want to overcompensate for what the child has missed out on but we need to keep a reality check on this and think about how much the child will actually appreciate, or use, the item we are going to buy.

Last but not least, have a good honest look at your home and contents. It may be that you gleefully added white carpets and leather sofas once your children left home. Children who have experienced trauma can often also damage items which do not belong to them and may seem to have little regard for the possessions of others. How robust is your furniture?

9E: What About My Pension?

As we all know, government guidelines are subject to change, and what may be correct today may not hold true in the future. The same can be said for private and state pensions and the effects this has on pension credits. Therefore, checking your entitlements before taking on any legal order is crucial. As the saying goes, you may be given something in one hand, but it could be taken away from the other. Here are some questions we are frequently asked at Kinship Carers UK.

Question: Can you claim a pension if you're a connected foster carer, retired or semi-retired?
In the UK, a default or forced retirement age no longer exists. This means you can continue working and claim your pension. You can foster and claim your pension or a state pension if you've reached the state pension age, currently 66. For a private pension, you can continue to foster and receive your pension on the condition you've reached the age you've agreed with your provider.

Question: What will be the impact if I become a special guardian and claim a pension?
Your benefits as a special guardian will not be impacted. You will also be exempt from the under-occupancy tax, and the benefit cap does not apply to you either. Also, if you are a special guardian and claim pension benefits, you will be eligible to receive child benefits or universal credits.

Question: What is Pension Credit?
Pension Credit is an additional benefit to your state pension, which is available for people of state pension age (currently 66) or older. It is a means-tested benefit that provides financial assistance to help with day-to-day expenses, including caring for a child. Pension Credit is designed to supplement your income

by providing an extra amount to those with a low income. The amount of Pension Credit you receive will depend on your overall household income. If you or your partner are over pension age, all fostering allowances, Special Guardianship Allowances, Child Arrangement Order allowances or Residence Order allowances are completely ignored when the pension credit is worked out.

Question: Can I claim other benefits?
Pensioners with dependent children (who are not foster children) can claim child benefits in the same way as other carers can. Pension Credit also includes a child element, equivalent to Child Tax Credit.

The Department for Work and Pensions disregards any Special Guardianship Allowance you receive from the local authority as part of your income if you claim means-tested benefits.

We recommend contacting the Citizens Advice Bureau or the Department for Work and Pensions for current benefits advice, which will help you consider the welfare benefits and financial issues specific to your circumstances.

9F: Childcare Costs and Support

Eve is a single grandmother who works full time as a senior manager. Children's Services asked Eve to take on her three-year-old grandson Carl under an interim care order while waiting for the SGO. Eve showed the local authority that all her income was accounted for with expenses like mortgage, car, bills, and so on. Her income was substantial, but her outgoings were too, and her finances would not cover the cost of childcare for her grandson. Eve requested financial support towards the nursery fees, and after some negotiation, the local authority agreed to pay until her grandson started school. Eve also included in her SGO support plan that the local authority would pay for holiday clubs and wrap-around care, which they agreed to cover.

There is government help with childcare costs for carers regardless of the kinship order. Whether you have toddlers or teens, you could get support. It is essential that you keep an eye on the government website for updates on childcare support. These websites will give you up-to-date details about how and when to register for support with childcare costs:

- England: www.childcarechoices.gov.uk
- Wales: www.gov.wales/help-paying-childcare
- Scotland: www.mygov.scot/childcare-costs-help.

Who needs permission?

SGO: The benefit of being a kinship carer with an SGO is that you have overall parental responsibility; therefore, you do not need to ask permission from the local authority or birth parents when considering childcare of any description.

CAO or private arrangements: For kinship carers with other orders or private arrangements, you must notify the birth parents as you may need their consent for major decisions about their care; this also depends on your agreement with them.

Connected foster carer: Depending on your local authority policy, permission must be sought from the children's social worker and/or parents if you are considering childcare, especially if it is longer than 24 hours. Also, arrangements for babysitting and regular childcare may have to be written into the Placement Plan. You may not be allowed to leave your foster child with babysitters/childminders if Children's Services has not approved them to be an adult in your support network. You may have to adhere to specific rules, such as babysitters must be at least 18 years of age.

If your child's social worker has not informed the childcare provider that your child is looked after, you must tell them when you register and provide them with your social worker's contact details.

For guidance on how to choose a childminder or childcare, visit these useful websites:

- www.nct.org.uk/life-parent/work-and-childcare/childcare/finding-childminder-all-you-need-know
- www.familyandchildcaretrust.org/five-steps-choosing-childcare
- www.childcare.co.uk/information/choosing-the-right-childcare.

CHAPTER 10

Making a Plan

Overview

A support plan is the most important consideration for all kinship carers before making a final choice of legal route, be it an SGO or a CAO. The most crucial thing to remember from this chapter is that in order to avoid future complications (including changes in local authority or government policies), you need a support plan that is:

- detailed
- comprehensive
- robust
- water-tight
- unchangeable.

Without such a plan, you risk facing significant problems, challenges and disappointments. We want all kinship carers to know they can seek support from the local authority if Children's Services are involved, regardless of the potential legal order.

Dom and Vanessa were employed full-time when they were approached to take on two kinship children. They had three children of their own and lived in a four-bedroom house; they went on holiday each year, went out for occasional meals, had their own cars, and comfortably managed their bills. They knew that taking on two extra children they had not planned for would not be financially manageable. The local authority helped pay towards a loft conversion for the two children. They provided bedroom furniture and all the necessary items they needed. Vanessa was paid an allowance for the children, which was very much needed as she soon found out that it was too difficult to look after two traumatized children and work full time. Both children required therapeutic support to overcome the trauma of their past, and their robust support plan meant that the children did not have to wait years to get the support they needed. Vanessa also received the necessary training, which was specific to their circumstances. Vanessa says:

> The support plan has helped us provide a loving, normal environment for the children, and they can participate in the same activities that our children experienced. The extra educational support the children received has also allowed them to fulfil their potential, and they are both doing well; the ongoing therapy has helped us all, and I am confident they will be well-rounded adults and have a great future because of the support plan Kinship Carers UK helped us acquire.

10A: What Is an SGO Support Plan?

The SGO support plan is an essential document for ensuring the future support needs of your kinship child, and the stability going forward. Before the Special Guardianship Order is granted, you and your local authority must agree on the robust support plan, which will be presented in court alongside the SGO. The *Special*

Guardianship Guidance outlines the type of support you and your child may require up to 18, 21 (end of education) or 25, if your child has additional needs.

Considering these recommendations and ensuring that the SGO support plan is comprehensive and well thought out is essential. You not only need to look at the current needs of your child now but also think about long-term considerations, such as contact/family time, therapy, health, education, training and future needs. We understand it isn't easy to see future needs, so we recommend you join Kinship Carers UK support groups, speak to carers at different stages of their kinship journey and learn about their experiences.

Valerie joined the Kinship Carers UK virtual support groups and booked in for the one-to-one support plan meeting. She says:

> I joined the support group specifically to learn about support plans; wow, it was mind-blowing. I started my kinship journey naively, thinking I knew everything I needed to know. I met some fantastic kinship carers from various backgrounds, knowledge and experiences. I enjoyed it so much that I still pop in occasionally. I then applied for the one-to-one SGO support plan session, which lasted just over an hour. We discussed everything, even things I had not thought about. My plan was then emailed to me to adjust if necessary, and I then gave it to my solicitor, who was amazed as she had not seen such a detailed plan before. The plan was then put into the format for court and handed to the local authority and judge. It was accepted, except there was a little battle over the finances, but this was sorted amicably. We owe a great thank you to everyone involved in making our future secure.

Kinship Carers UK provides confidential, informative support to help you understand your entitlements to an SGO support plan. It asks only for a small voluntary contribution. You are encouraged to use any funds your local authority provides to have a solicitor make your support plan watertight.

Do check your house and contents insurance. Some policies include family legal expenses, which could cover the cost of professional advice and representation.

10B: What Should Be in an SGO Support Plan?

The SGO support plan is unique to your kinship child and your personal circumstances. There is no one-size-fits-all plan. But every carer needs to consider current circumstances and long-term commitments for the future. None of us has a clear insight into the future. However, there are firm essentials you will need to take into consideration, such as health, finances, education and family time.

It is important to ensure that your SGO support plan is comprehensive and complies with all guidelines. The following are some areas to focus on that will help ensure your plan is successful:

- Activities for the child/ren
- Behavioural, social and emotional development
- Counselling, advice and information
- Educational support
- Family time/contact arrangements, assistance and mediation
- Financial support
- Health needs, including any special needs which a disabled child may have or significant medical needs
- Housing and accommodation
- Legal applications
- Leaving care
- Support Services and subscriptions – NATP membership,

training and advice for all families of children who have suffered developmental trauma
- Therapeutic needs
- Physical health needs.

If you require additional assistance, Kinship Carers UK can offer one-to-one meetings, which can be scheduled by visiting www.kinshipcarersuk.com/contact.

10C: Help With Accommodation

If required, the local authority can provide financial assistance to ensure the child is well cared for. This may include the provision of furniture such as bedroom furniture and bedding, and household equipment such as white goods, a fridge, a freezer and a washing machine. The local authority may also make necessary adjustments to the home, such as an extension, loft conversion or a garden pod to provide additional space. We advise that these discussions are recorded and acted on before the order is granted, as many kinship carers and their families live in cramped, overcrowded conditions. There is little room for negotiation once the SGO or CAO is awarded.

Alvita is a single-parent carer and lives in a two-bedroom flat with her daughter and kinship nephew Oskar. Alvita took in her nephew without hesitation and gave him her bedroom, believing it was short term; nine months later, her local authority provided her with finance to buy a bed settee as the housing shortage meant they were continually pushed down the list. It took six years to move to a three-bedroom apartment, despite support from their social worker. Looking back, Alvita would not have changed her actions as she believed this was the best for her nephew.

Andy and Joao have a two-bedroom house and were asked to take on their 16-year-old nephew; they told the local authority they could not accommodate him as they did not have the physical space and could not alter the house. The local authority offered to provide their nephew with a self-contained pod with a bedroom, bathroom and living space placed in their garden. This allowed their nephew close supervision, support and a space of his own.

If you are a tenant of the housing authority and you need a bigger house, the local authority may be able to help you relocate. However, it's important to remember that this process may come with challenges and a long waiting period due to the high demand for social housing. You may have to continue to live in your current home for a very long time.

To find out more about housing visit:

- www.citizensadvice.org.uk/housing
- www.sheltercymru.org.uk.

You can also search for your local council details at www.gov.uk/find-local-council.

10D: Support Plan: Finances

[See also 9B: Entitlements]

If you are considering becoming a special guardian, please accept the financial support that is available to help you provide the best possible care for your kinship child. This support ensures that you have the resources to meet your kinship child's needs, such as clothing, essentials and equipment, and allow them to pursue hobbies and activities that will mean they have a fulfilled life.

Sometimes, children require additional support due to illness, disability, emotional or behavioural challenges, or past abuse or neglect. In these cases, it may be necessary to request increased financial support.

It's important to clarify that financial assistance sometimes does not cover remuneration (wage element) for special guardians caring for kinship children. However, suppose you were a kinship foster carer and received remuneration while fostering the child. In that case, the local authority may continue to provide that assistance for up to two years following the Special Guardianship Order. If you require further financial assistance beyond the initial two-year period, it must be clearly stated and agreed on in the support plan. This ensures that you, as a kinship carer, receive the financial support you and your child deserve.

In some cases, kinship carers do not have legal representation or cannot afford it. If you are in such a situation, you can ask the local authority to consider contributing to the legal costs associated with making a Special Guardianship Order, including the support plan and court fees. Some local authorities may pay for a solicitor to review the plan and make any necessary improvements to ensure it is reliable and there is no chance of any misunderstandings.

The contentious question you may ask is: How much will I receive for raising a kinship child? Currently, there is no fixed amount unless you are living in Scotland. Each local authority has its own rules and you can look them up on their website. Also, local authority payments can alter from case to case, even within the same local authority. To find out what you could be entitled to, ask the local authority for their kinship friends and family policy and ask them for the direct answer in writing. Please remember that these payments can be negotiated and altered unless locked into your support plan.

Financial support for a special guardian ceases when the kinship child reaches 18 years of age unless there is an agreement in the support plan stating otherwise. Support may also end if your kinship child moves out of your home, completes full-time education or training and begins employment, or qualifies for Universal Credit on their own.

10E: Overcoming Obstacles

[See also 1I: Where Can I Go for Help?]

Enza Smith writes: Sometimes I find myself thinking, 'if only'. In hindsight, I could have saved myself a lot of stress, time, struggles – the list can go on. So here is some advice that will save you a lot of stress in the future:

- Get the support plan right in the first place.
- Lock it down.
- Negotiate hard now.
- Push back now, even if you think you will not get anywhere.
- Make your case to the professionals, including social workers and CAFCASS officers.

This support plan, this next chapter in your life, this legal order, will change the lives of everyone around you, and the kinship child. It is a legal order set until the child is 18 or older. View it as a contract. Don't accept anything less than what you need, when the stakes are as crucial as a child's future pathway to adult life! Your decisions now will affect lives. It's in your hands.

If you find negotiating difficult, ask someone to advocate on your behalf or put it in an email. Please do not sit there and say they know best, because they do not. Do not leave your support plan open to changes you are unaware of. There are organizations to reach out to and professionals to ask.

If you have accepted a support plan or have left it open to

change, please remember that you are entitled to dispute it, state your case and request an assessment of the need. If the local authority wishes to modify or remove anything from the plan, they must first inform you as the special guardian and allow you to express your thoughts formally. This should ensure that any changes to the support plan align with your kinship child's needs and yours as the special guardian.

To reassure you, if you have had an SGO in place for three years and you move home to another area, your new local authority will take over the responsibility of assessing and providing support services for you and your kinship child. However, it's important to note that the original local authority will still be responsible for assessing and providing financial support.

Remember, you are not alone; there are independent services that can help you navigate. We have listed them in 1I: Where Can I Go for Help?

CHAPTER 11

A New Life?

Overview

Do you find yourself thinking, 'It's all over'? With new beginnings come endings. We now have to settle into a way of life where everything looks different from how it used to look. We are now having to think about how we manage our relationships with the child's birth parents for the long term. This can be made difficult as we consider ways to improve and maintain visits for the child.

Although we have new stresses and worries around different ways of managing communication and relationships, we also need to keep an open mind about changes that are going to happen. You know logically that your children will grow. You know logically that life will change. But sometimes it can feel a bit like Groundhog Day and there is always the threat of legal challenges coming at you when you least expect it. It's much better to be open to this and aware of these issues rather than being caught unawares. There might be new titles to consider. You may be 'Granny' but you're definitely fulfilling the 'Mum' role. Perhaps you are 'Uncle' but the child wants to call you 'Dad'. How do you balance that? This chapter will help you with all of that.

11A: Managing Communication

[See also Chapter 5: Family Tensions, Visits and Family Time (Contact)]

Enza Smith writes: As things begin to settle down, it's very likely that your connected child will be seeing other members of the extended family and birth parents. If you're not careful, it can feel as if your life has been taken over by the birth parents. This is very difficult, as the birth parent is likely to be a daughter, son, sister, brother or some other close relative or friend.

If the parent has now lost custody of their child, the next best thing for them is to be in constant communication with you! This is not going to work. Your connected child is now being parented by you and you have to claim the child. You have to help the child to feel a proper part of your family. This is difficult to do if you're getting constant FaceTime requests, voice messages or other messages from the child's other relatives.

You need to put in some boundaries. One thing you can do is to get a different phone which you only use for arranging visits with birth family and other members of the child's extended family. In this way, you're not constantly inundated with messages. You can be clear with the child's birth parents that you will not be responding to messages from them, outside what has been prescribed by the court.

This can be incredibly difficult where there is animosity. If you are lucky, you may have managed to preserve your relationship and everything is very cordial. But beware, if you decide to keep using your original phone and have a more relaxed approach to making arrangements, this can deteriorate rapidly. Be prepared to make the changes you need to make, and put in the boundaries that you need to put in.

You can also insist that arrangements are made via email so

that everything is in writing and very clearly understood. This is useful if you have a parent who insists that arrangements have been changed or not kept to. You do not want to give anyone ammunition with which to go back to court, and confusion around visits and contact is a surefire way to do that.

As a connected or kinship carer, you may well feel that you are in a difficult situation where you are continuing to provide support and care to the birth parent of the child. Sometimes it can be useful to divide this up and separate out the time. In my situation, I made sure there were specific times when I saw my daughter, away from supervising the visits. We also maintained a chatty conversation where we spoke about anything apart from her son. In this way, links were maintained but boundaries were not crossed.

11B: Keeping an Open Mind

Nothing stays the same forever.

During the time when your connected child first came to you with all the assessments and legal procedures going on, anxieties and feelings were heightened. There may well have been a lot of anger, resentment and blame around. However, it takes a lot of energy to maintain anger and resentment over a long period of time.

It's true that your relationship with the child's birth parents may never be quite the same, but it will change over time. People adapt to the new normal and sometimes they are even able to acknowledge that the best decisions were made for the child.

It's important to keep an open mind and be aware of changes that are happening. If the court has left decisions largely in the family's hands (about changes for the future around visits), then this is something that you may have some flexibility with.

Obviously you cannot do anything that would put the child at risk or would make them feel unhappy or frightened, but perhaps there may come a time where family days out again become possible, and everyone has a nice time.

Be alert to these possibilities and these changes. It may feel as if they are a very long way off now, but when we think about parents who have divorced amid a lot of animosity, we do see that in a few years that bad feeling is significantly reduced and there's often reciprocal and cooperative co-parenting happening. The same can happen in kinship situations.

The best outcome for the child in a kinship situation is to maintain a positive view of themselves and to be able to have as positive a relationship as possible with their birth parents, whenever that is safe. By being alert to positive change, we can help the child to view their lives and their early childhood in a more constructive way.

11C: Legal Challenges

[See also 1F: Court Glossary and Who You May See in Court, Chapter 10: Making a Plan]

Kinship care is seen as the best outcome for children, despite all the heartache of getting to what feels like a stable place for you and the kinship child. However, it can become a bumpy legal road for some carers, with many more court appearances. At this point, we want to remind you that connected foster care, SGOs and CAOs are not permanent orders and can be legally challenged at any time. If birth parents have enough reason to vary an SGO, they can apply to the courts. This can put an enormous strain on the kinship family as the parent's wants or demands may not always align with the child's best interests.

SGOs can also be discharged. A birth parent can *only* apply for an SGO to be overturned where the court has granted permission for the application because the parent has demonstrated a significant change in circumstances.

> Tracey and Mark are connected foster carers. Their daughter suffered from severe postnatal depression after the birth of her first child, but after three years, she feels she has fully recovered. Their daughter has moved to weekend family time and feels she can build up to having her child back over the next six months. Children's Services are happy, and Tracey and Mark are pleased to work on a shared care agreement; this is the plan until their grandchild returns home. They still have their grandchild back for sleepovers and are able to live a more normal life. Children's Services will return this case to court to discharge the order, and Tracey and Mark will not be required to attend.

> The children's birth parents feel aggrieved that their children were removed from them because of drug and substance misuse, harm and neglect. Throughout the court process for the SGO, they had not entirely accepted the consequences of their behaviour. Now the social workers have gone, the parents have shifted the blame to Donna for keeping their children away from them. They feel that they should see the children as often as they wish. They say things like, 'They are our children', 'We can do as we want now, we are out of court, and social workers are now gone', 'We want more contact now, so we are taking you to court!'

Having an SGO gives kinship carers parental responsibility. Therefore, you may be entitled to legal aid if you satisfy the criteria. Hiring a solicitor might not be feasible for everyone. But don't worry; you still have options. You can choose to represent yourself, and the court will guide you. If it's deemed safe, you might be asked to attend mediation with the birth parents to find a solution that works for everyone. If you feel uncomfortable in the same room, don't hesitate to let the mediator know. You can also request a children's advocate to present the children's wishes and feelings to the court. Everyone must agree that the decisions made should prioritize the child's best interests.

11D: Managing the Expectations of Others

(See also 5B: Blame and Judgement)

Enza Smith writes: Managing parental expectations during family celebrations, such as birthdays, weddings and funerals, can be challenging at the best of times. At these events, birth parents may conveniently forget that you are the primary carer for their child or do not want other people to know their failings or inadequacies, which can lead to conflicts, tension and emotional turmoil for the child. One important lesson I learned is that it's crucial to establish clear roles, boundaries and expectations before any event to avoid any misunderstandings, arguments and the dreaded fallout.

My grandson and I were invited to a family wedding, and I was surprised that my daughter and her partner, who had not seen their son for a couple of years, were also going. I explained to my grandson that his parents would be at the wedding with other family members and that he would be seeing them for a while. He would be safe and coming home with me as normal. However, what I did not factor in was that his parents would try and move back to a temporary role as parents for everyone to see. They wanted to show everyone that they were his loving parents, and they showered attention on him for a while. This led to blurred boundaries and emotional conflicts, challenging for my grandson and me. But like some parents who have limited understanding of their child's emotional needs, he was soon ignored and rejected, and they returned to being strangers in his life once again.

I had to step in and physically remove my grandson from this emotional roller coaster, stabilize him the best I could and compose myself. I decided to leave the wedding early. It took over a whole week for my grandson to recover emotionally.

I have learned to establish more precise boundaries and expectations from the birth parents, which has led to a better understanding of our roles. These are some of the strategies I have learned that may help you:

- **Communicate** calmly and clearly before the event. This can minimize any misunderstanding of boundaries and expectations.
- **Set manageable expectations:** When it comes to parenting a kinship child, setting realistic and achievable expectations is vital. While parents may have a desire to spend more time with their children, everyone must work together in the best interests of the child. If that means managing or limiting parental expectations, then it is necessary to do so.
- **Be prepared to negotiate** but do not compromise on the child's best interests. 'You can spend time with us at the wedding; however, this is what we will do to make this a good day.'
- **Make no assumptions** that birth parents will comply in public settings. Therefore, it's a good idea to plan an exit strategy.

I ensured that my grandson was never put in this position again, which has led him to be the well-rounded man he is today.

11E: Who Am I Now?

[See also 3C: A Different Parent, 6B: Ways of
Communicating the Child's Story]

It can be difficult navigating the changing roles in our lives. It may be that you have been a parent for a number of years and then rediscovered what it feels like to have a bit more freedom. Or perhaps you are an aunt or uncle with a young family of your own and your family has become extended.

Whatever your role, having a connected child come to join you is going to change that. If you have been in a grandparent role for this child, you're suddenly doing the parenting role, but you're still 'Granny' or 'Grandad'. If your child is very young and you have other children living with you, your connected child is likely to learn their language. What happens when they start calling you 'Mummy' or 'Daddy' and simply copying your children?

Discussions and decisions need to be made about this kind of thing. We can't just wander into our new role and hope it will all stay the same, because it doesn't. Although of course we are always going to make sure the child knows the truth about their circumstances. It may be that they do not want to feel different to other children at school. This is a fine balancing act!

The best approach is always one of honesty. By giving simple explanations to the child and others close to you, you can avoid lots of confusing or embarrassing situations. We must also take into account the feelings of the birth parent. Perhaps you are still in a parent role with your son or daughter living at home and are parenting their child alongside. This can also be confusing for your connected child.

In 6B: Ways of Communicating the Child's Story, we looked at the importance of life story work and the child's narrative. This section also helped with terminology to use with the child to help to separate out roles.

In all of this, remember that you are still *you*. Keep some things back which are just about you and just about your own identity. This might be hobbies, friendships and social activities. In kinship care, our tasks can change from week to week or it can certainly feel like that! Make sure that you keep your feet on the ground.

CHAPTER 12

Growing and Leaving

Overview

Well, nothing *does* stay the same forever and of course the children we are caring for will grow up. We might dread this; we might look forward to it. Whatever, it *will* happen. We might have thought that the days of looking after teenagers were behind us but now we're facing them again. Or perhaps we suddenly have a lot more young adults around than we thought we were going to have. We might be facing those dreaded teenage years for the second time around, but this time, perhaps our health is not so good and we're feeling a bit older or a bit more tired. How do we manage that challenge? This chapter looks at how we might plan to get the help we need as we age, especially where our children have lots of energy. It will also consider how things may change in the future – legal changes, visits with birth family and also, of course, as children become older they can vote with their feet.

We know that children who have experienced trauma are often less emotionally mature than others, so we need to think about how we will prepare our children for independence with that in the background. Last but not least, we need to think about what we can and cannot change, and how we can stay in the background for our children – even when it can be really tough.

12A: Caring for Teens

[See also 1I: Where Can I Go for Help?]

Teenagers are like Marmite; you either like them or loathe them! Humour aside, we all know it can be the most challenging time for them. Caring for teens can be more complicated for kinship carers due to several reasons, not including the normal changes teens have to put up with, such as hormones and emotional and body changes. The added extra concerns, such as their experience of trauma, will make it worse. Or you may feel you are under more scrutiny than you were with your own children, as you feel as if you are being judged, especially if it was your child who was the birth parent that caused the reason for your grandchild to be living with you. Or you may have concerns about generational differences, such as changes in society since you were a teenager, like social media, phones and communication overload, not to mention new levels of peer pressure. Or your teenager is emotionally vulnerable, and others take advantage of it. We could go on, but we won't. Take it from us who have been there: you can only do your best. As one young man says:

> Being raised by my nan has saved me. If it was not for her, I would be in prison by now. She has taught me how to behave and the difference between right and wrong, not to lie, to treat people with respect, and to treat others how you want to be treated. Don't get me wrong, I was not perfect. I bent many rules, and I was a bit of a pain and made mistakes, but she forgave me and encouraged me to learn from my mistakes. She would forgive me, always say, let's move on and draw a line in the sand, as tomorrow is another day.

It's understandable that sometimes, despite your best efforts, you may find it challenging to connect with your teenager, or they continually kick the boundary fence close to disrepair. It can be disheartening to see your child turn away, go against the safety net you have put up for them, vote with their feet or secretly connect with the very people that they were removed from.

Helpful tips

- Communicate openly and honestly with your teen, take the time to listen, and ask a family member or friend to help.
- Take time out, if you feel out of control or angry – walk away and discuss the issues later.
- Don't be dragged into an argument – realize when this happens and don't engage.
- Focus on a stable environment – re-establish boundaries, reassess house rules and respect their need for their own space and alone time.
- Create a family bonding time and find activities that bring you together.
- Join a support group and talk to others.
- Remember that it's okay to feel overwhelmed and unsure how to proceed – know you're not alone.

The support networks in 1I: Where Can I Go for Help? can help you to navigate complex emotions during this challenging time. Together, we can find a way to move forward and provide the best support possible.

12B: Am I Too Old for This?

Christine and John are great-grandparents who are responsible for their granddaughter under a Special Guardianship Order. Christine says:

Age is just a number when it comes to being a kinship carer. You can do it successfully if you have the desire and physical ability. You also need to be aware of your limitations, such as the physical, mental, health demands and energy it takes to keep up with a little one. Also, it's important to keep in mind that kinship keeps you poor. We only get a little SGO allowance on top of our pensions, and life is tight.

Christine has a supportive husband, and they all enjoy spending time together and have a family to turn to when needed. The biggest challenge for Christine is dealing with the issues that arise from the birth parents; 'It's not just taking on your grandchild, but it's dealing with the nonsense that comes with it.'

Christine has a good support network, which is essential for older caregivers to consider. In addition, her granddaughter has family members who will take care of her if the time comes when her grandparents can no longer provide care.

Sarah is a grandmother kinship carer, an inspiring lady who fostered her grandson after his mother was imprisoned. Sarah had been fit and healthy. However, the natural ageing process has slowed her down, and she now needs walking aids. Sarah believes the age and ability of older carers are subjective as each individual's situation differs. She made the noble decision to become a connected foster kinship carer at the age of 64 because she didn't want her grandchild to grow up in foster care with strangers. Sarah gets very tired, 'I get very stressed sometimes. Friends tell me to rest and make time for myself, but where? When?' Sarah is understandably concerned about what would happen if she became very ill, as she does not want her grandson to become her carer.

Sarah spends as much enjoyable time with her grandson

as possible and makes many memories with him. She has to pace herself these days because she gets tired quickly, but thankfully, her grandson loves playing football with his friends, which helps keep him active. Sarah's story exemplifies selflessness and love; we can all learn from her experiences.

Child and adult services need to work together to ensure that kinship carers have access to independent sources of support. This will help in providing the necessary assistance and care for the children. In many cases, placing a child with a grandparent could be a better option than placing them in foster care. Ultimately, it is your decision. No one should judge you for it; you must do what is right for you and be realistic about what you can provide and ask for help if you feel you need it.

12C: Preparing for Independence

[See also 4E: Teaching Cause and Effect]

Sarah Naish writes: When your children reach their late teens they may well be thinking about leaving home. You might embrace this idea with enthusiasm and glee! On the other hand, you might read this and be extremely worried about how they are going to manage to live independently.

Some children who have experienced trauma tend to mature at a slower rate and may not be ready to leave home at the same age as their peers. They may require significant support to live independently. Additionally, if they struggle with understanding the relationship between actions and consequences and prioritize immediate gratification, it can greatly affect their ability to budget effectively.

If you're lucky, your adult child will accept your help with budgeting, but often this is not the case. We need to allow natural consequences to occur, and be ready to help when things go wrong, but not necessarily by bailing them out financially. I used to help my adult children by getting them food and making sure their home was okay. I quickly learned that if I gave them money it would be spent on the latest phone or something useless that wouldn't keep them warm at night!

When our children leave home or are preparing to leave home, it doesn't necessarily mean everything is going to be okay. Naturally, some of our adult kinship children may gravitate back towards their birth parents, and this comes with its own raft of problems. We have to be honest with ourselves and clear about what we can and cannot change.

As your adult connected children spend less time at home, you need to ensure that you take some time to rest, reflect and plan. It can be easy to get carried away with negative thoughts and excessive planning. However, you may need to learn to step back; and it may mean doing so at a different pace than you would have for a securely attached child. You may need to be realistic and assess what you can and cannot change.

12D: Know What You Can Change

Sarah Naish writes: As our adult children move more towards independence, naturally there may be a lot of difficulties which occur. It may be that we cling on to old ways and try to influence and change what is happening. Nevertheless, we have to be really careful about differentiating between letting go and giving up.

When we let our children go, and allow them to spread their wings, we are waiting nearby and watching carefully to see if we are needed. This is very different to feeling as if we can't help them any more and giving up on them. This is a very lonely place to be for you and for your adult child too. Be careful not to close the pathway back. Children who have suffered trauma, even as young adults, may well still suffer the devastating effects of toxic shame. This can make it really difficult for them to admit they have made a mistake, or to ask for help. You have to be the one to throw the ladder down the 'shame pit'! They aren't going to ask you.

As living arrangements change, it can be a very useful task to separate out into a physical list, what you *can* change and what you *can't* change. For example, if your adult child has decided to stay out late night after night and not come home, although you can put in therapeutic parenting strategies to help them to make better choices, you can't actually control what they are doing. This is even more the case when they are over 18 and are trying to make their way in the world. This is a natural progression, but it can be extremely worrying when our children are much less mature than other young people of 18+.

Often, we find that some of the bigger changes happen with our children around the age of 25. This may feel like a very long way off. I certainly noticed with all my children, much higher levels of maturity and reflection around this age. Everything got easier from this point on.

There is no shame in taking a step back, reassuring your adult child that you are there for them, but you want them to try to make some decisions on their own. Make clear that you are there for support and help and advice, but you're not necessarily going to carry on doing everything.

Naturally, there is a difference here where you have a child who is perhaps incapable of living independently. In these circumstances, you have to be brave and face long-term planning. You need to think about:

- who is going to be there for the child when you can't be
- making a will
- making long-term financial arrangements

- perhaps creating a semi-independent living space within your own home.

Remember, you deserve time for *you* as well. There is no rule that says that when you become a kinship carer, you then have to dedicate the rest of your life to being a full-time carer.

Afterword

Enza Smith writes: Experience the rewards of being a kinship carer!

This book discusses the various challenges of being a kinship carer. However, I would like to conclude on a positive note by sharing some of the joys of this role. As a kinship carer, I have had the privilege of watching my grandson grow from infant to teenager and then to adulthood. Although the journey has had its ups and downs, I have experienced many more moments of happiness. I am proud to have played a role in changing my grandson's life's path and taking him from a difficult start to a successful point in life. I have been a witness to Bradley's growth and development into a wonderful, compassionate and hardworking man. All the hard work has paid off, and he has excelled academically and professionally. His future is bright, and he is a true success story. Despite the difficulties, being a kinship carer has been completely worth it. Being a kinship carer has been a defining experience that has taught me the importance of perseverance and the rewards of hard work. Bradley's success story is a testament to the fact that with dedication and support, if our kinship children are able to choose to do so, they can overcome their difficulties and achieve their dreams.

Sarah Naish writes: As Enza and I have written this book and reflected on our shared experiences, it has made us realize how important this book was to write. There are so many of you who are struggling alone and perhaps wondering what to do next. We both sincerely hope that this book has been your guiding light and companion, and that you now know where you can go for help to assist you in your critically important journey, which will allow your children to heal and to live their best life. Our children bring us challenges and worry, but they also give us another chance to get things right, laughter, love and a sense of reward.

Know that we appreciate you – and know that your struggle does not go unseen.

References

Ottaway, H. & Selwyn, J. (2016). *'No-one told us it was going to be like this':
Compassion fatigue and foster carers*. The Hadley Centre for Adoption
and Foster Care Studies, Bristol University.

Naish, S. (2016). *William Wobbly and the Very Bad Day*. Jessica Kingsley
Publishers.

Naish, S. (2018). *Rosie Rudey and the Enormous Chocolate Mountain*. Jessica
Kingsley Publishers.

Naish, S. (2018). *The A–Z of Therapeutic Parenting*. Jessica Kingsley
Publishers.

Naish, S. (2022). *The A–Z of Survival Strategies: From Chaos to Cake*. Jessica
Kingsley Publishers.

Naish, S., Oakley, A., O'Brien, H., Penna, S. & Thrower, D. (2023). *The A–Z
of Trauma-Informed Teaching*. Jessica Kingsley Publishers.

*Trauma Informed Preparation and Assessment Connected/Kinship (TIPPACK)
with integrated training*. (2024). www.inspiretraininggroup.com/
qualifications

Current underpinning legislation in the UK can be found at:

- Children Act 1989: family and friends care
  www.legislationgov.uk
- The Special Guardianship Regulations 2005
  www.legislation.gov.uk
- The Special Guardianship (Amendment) Regulations 2016
  www.legislation.gov.uk